THE COMPLETE GUIDE TO SERVICE LINE MARKETING

KAREN CORRIGAN

HCPro

The Complete Guide to Service Line Marketing is published by HealthLeaders Media.

 5 4 3 2 1

ISBN: 978-1-60146-752-2

HCPro, Inc., provides information resources for the healthcare industry.

HCPro, Inc., is not affiliated in any way with The Joint Commission, which owns the JCAHO and Joint Commission trademarks.

Karen Corrigan, Author
Carrie Vaughan, Editor
Rick Johnson, Executive Editor
Matt Cann, Group Publisher
Doug Ponte, Cover Designer
Janell Lukac, Graphic Artist
Leah Jenness, Copyeditor
Alison Forman, Proofreader
Matt Sharpe, Production Supervisor
Susan Darbyshire, Art Director
Jean St. Pierre, Senior Director of Operations

Advice given is general. Readers should consult professional counsel for specific legal, ethical, or clinical questions.

Arrangements can be made for quantity discounts. For more information, contact:

HCPro, Inc.
75 Sylvan Street, Suite A-101
Danvers, MA 01923
Telephone: 800/650-6787 or 781/639-1872
Fax: 800/639-8511
E-mail: *customerservice@hcpro.com*

HCPro, Inc., is the parent company of HealthLeaders Media

Visit HCPro at its World Wide Web sites:
***www.healthleadersmedia.com*, *www.healthleadersmedia.com/marketing*,**
www.hcpro.com*, and *www.hcmarketplace.com

Rev. 12/2012
52223

Contents

About the Author

Karen Corrigan

Karen Corrigan is an author and speaker on health industry trends, competitive strategy, brand building, and strategic marketing. She is a leading proponent for value innovation in the healthcare industry. In 2007, Karen founded and launched the Innovator's Studio to provide a unique forum where chief marketing and chief strategy officers can discover, create, and adopt market-leading ideas and strategies.

Today, Karen provides counsel on competitive positioning, brand, growth, and marketing strategies to health systems, businesses, and service organizations. Recently, she was chief strategy officer for Navvis & Company, a St. Louis-based consultancy providing planning, physician alignment, leadership, and performance strategies to health systems and physician organizations. In 1998, Karen founded and served as CEO of The Strategy Group, a management consultancy that merged with Navvis & Company in 2008.

Before embarking on her consulting career, she held the position of vice president for system development at Sentara Healthcare in Norfolk, Virginia, and she also worked with Riverside Health System and Winchester Medical Center in Virginia.

Karen is a member of the Forum for Healthcare Strategists, American College of Healthcare Executives, Society for Healthcare Strategy and Market Development, and Virginia Press Women. She hosts and writes for Chief Marketing Officer *(www.karencorrigan.com),* a blog for healthcare marketing executives.

Acknowledgments

I would like to acknowledge my healthcare colleagues, coworkers, clients, and friends as this body of work reflects the collective knowledge and experience gained through many years of working alongside thoughtful, intelligent people committed to building successful healthcare systems. Specifically, among them, the late Glenn Mitchell, former CEO of Sentara Healthcare in Norfolk, Virginia, who was a visionary mentor and advocate for the professional marketing discipline in the industry.

Thanks also go to the leadership and consultants of Navvis & Company in St. Louis, Missouri, for their encouragement and support for writing this book, as well as for the contribution of concepts, models, and material referenced throughout. Susan Lilly and Becky Barney-Villano aided significantly with research and interviews.

I am also grateful to the healthcare marketing and service line executives that contributed insights, information, and their valuable time to the book's case studies, including:

- Dana Allen and Steve Jenkins, Norton Healthcare, Louisville, Kentucky
- Tom Comes, Borgess Healthcare, Kalamazoo, Michigan
- Suzanne Hendery, Baystate Health System, Springfield, Massachusetts
- Chris Holt, Holy Redeemer Healthcare, Philadelphia, Pennsylvania

- Peggy Mika, Christiana Care, Wilmington, Delaware
- Jan Miller, St. Luke's Health System, Boise, Idaho
- Kim Menefee, Michelle Robinson, and Elaine Morgan, WellStar Healthcare, Marietta, Georgia
- Bill Munley, St. Francis Health System, Greenville, South Carolina
- Jaimie Somlai, Tesha Urban, and Steve Strohbusch, ProHealth Care, Milwaukee, Wisconsin

I would also like to thank Gienna Shaw, senior technology editor for HealthLeaders Media, who first approached me with the idea for this book. Her encouragement, along with that of Rick Johnson, and the steady, patient guidance of Carrie Vaughan, are much appreciated.

And, finally, thank you to my husband, Robin Cowherd, and children, Diron and Jody, Erin and Aaron, and Sarah, for your love and support.

Karen Corrigan

CHAPTER 1

Driving Growth Through Service Line Marketing

Since its inception nearly three decades ago, service line marketing has remained a primary focus for health systems seeking growth, profitability, and sustainable competitive advantage in a complex and rapidly evolving industry. In its earliest days, the discipline of marketing in hospitals was a fledging practice confronting the advent of market competition in a trade historically cast as public service.

Those first rudimentary attempts at service line marketing had one thing in common across markets and organizations: They were mostly about promotions. Consequently, hospitals experienced a mixed bag of results from their service line marketing investments. Marketers focused more on messaging reach and frequency than on positioning and differentiation. In their defense, administrators and physicians believed marketing to be a communications discipline rather than a core business competency. Thus, most service line marketing initiatives were overinvested in advertising and significantly underinvested in research, product development, customer service, brand building, channel strategies, marketing information systems, and other capabilities essential to driving strategic growth.

Throughout the 1980s, 1990s, and into this century, new competitive challenges emerged with increasing frequency in the healthcare industry, constantly reshaping the basis for competitive effectiveness. Rapid diffusion of clinical technologies into community hospital settings sparked a medical arms race as hospitals sought to be the first to market with new service line capabilities. Growth in managed care patients set off the first round of consolidation in the healthcare industry as hospitals sought contracting leverage through scale and market coverage. Impending physician shortages and unsustainable practice economics drove hospitals and doctors together into new integrated business arrangements. Emergence of retail health models disrupted conventional channels. And the Internet provided unprecedented access to information, resources, and commerce for a growing, graying population and increasingly informed proactive health consumers.

Now, with the passage of sweeping health reform legislation—the Patient Protection and Affordable Care Act of 2010 (amended by the Health Care and Education Reconciliation Act)—the basis of competition will once again evolve as health systems, service line leaders, and marketing executives embrace new demands for value and accountability.

More than ever, marketing is required as a core business discipline health systems need to achieve their desired service line growth objectives. Addressing the impact of value-based reimbursement models; engaging physicians organized in integrated structures; managing service line portfolios across markets and major lines of business; embracing online and social media environments; creating a pipeline of new, brand-driven products; and driving channel development and growth are all critical factors in successful service line marketing. To effectively compete in the marketplace, it is important for health systems to understand this new, more sophisticated approach.

Evolution of Clinical Service Lines

Clinical service line management emerged in the early 1980s when the inpatient prospective payment systems forced hospitals to look at services in new ways to better understand the impact of volume, revenue, and cost of specific programs on the overall financial performance of their institutions.

This required the creation of diagnosis-related groups (DRG)—or aggregated sets of services related to a category of primary diagnosis (e.g., heart disease), procedures (e.g., joint replacement), or need-based segments (e.g., pregnant women)—in order to evaluate clinical efficiency, business opportunity, and profitability.

As it became evident that certain types of patients and procedures contributed more to a positive bottom line than others, competition increased among hospitals for the more profitable business segments. In addition, healthcare institutions adopted the manufacturing industry's concepts of portfolio analysis and product line management.

The number of hospital marketing functions grew rapidly during the 1980s as health systems positioned themselves to more effectively grow service line volumes. Because healthcare organizations by and large did not consider themselves true "businesses" competing head to head for consumer preference and loyalty, these early marketing operations were often spin-offs of public relations or community outreach services and focused heavily on promotions. Thus, the first generation of service line strategies tended to be service line marketing versus service line management.

The popularity of service line management has ebbed and flowed over the past 30 years; this is attributed to a number of factors ranging from the changing nature of competition in the healthcare industry to misalignment of internal resources to variations in clinical practice to mixed financial results. Since its origin in the early 1980s, much has been debated about the structure, strategy, and capabilities of service line organizations.

Current and Emerging Service Line Structures

Service line management is an effective approach for focusing clinical strategies, organizing for effective delivery of care, generating growth, and creating competitive advantages for health systems and hospitals.

In general, the service line business model has evolved from service line marketing in the 1980s to clinical program operations in the 1990s to today's more systematic approach of managing a defined line of business delivering a bundle of services to distinct market segments (see Figure 1.1).

FIGURE 1.1

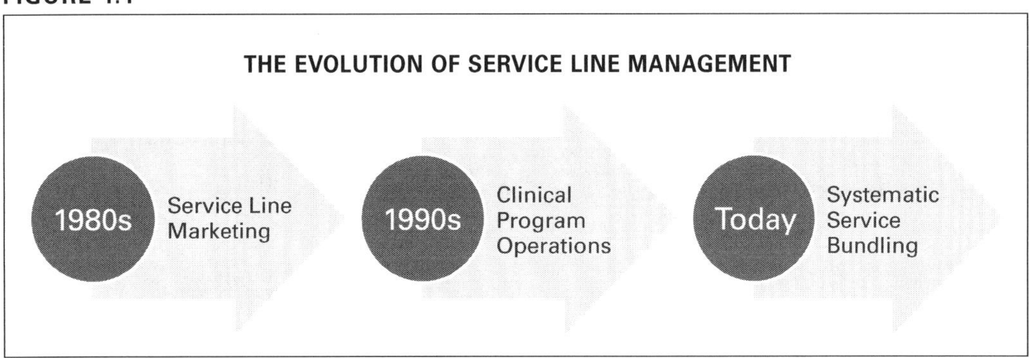

In practice, however, service line models differ widely across health systems and hospitals. There are multiple service line management structures, each characterized by different approaches to the market, different degrees of integration or service consolidation, and different degrees of centralization, delegation of authority, and functional specialization. Three common approaches are matrix, direct line, and comanagement structures.

Matrix structures

A matrix service line structure is typically led by an executive who has broad responsibility for setting overall strategic direction, managing service line growth, developing new programs, forging physician relationships, and achieving financial objectives. Other managers have service line responsibility for various functions required to deliver services. These include heads of clinical departments or units, such as nursing, pharmacy, imaging, and surgery, as well as of departments with administrative functions, such as marketing and finance.

Health systems composed of multiple hospitals may have matrix service line structures that span multiple facilities. Increasingly, these structures also include the continuum of inpatient, outpatient, and postacute services.

Matrix structures require significant coordination and collaboration across hospitals and systems.

Direct line structures

In direct line structures, an administrator has operating responsibility and accountability for the clinical departments that make up the service line, as well as for planning, clinical program development, and volume growth. The direct line leader often has a clinical background and business and management expertise. Under this structure, marketing, decision support, referral development, finance, and other similar functions provide support to the service line executive for business and administrative services—although there are hospitals where some of these functions are embedded in the service line structure. This approach may be more common in an academic medical center or hospital where core, related clinical programs are more closely aligned from programmatic, structural, and competency perspectives.

Clinical comanagement structures

Clinical comanagement is a service line structure gaining renewed interest from both hospitals and physician organizations. Under the comanagement arrangement, hospitals contract with an organized group of physicians to provide daily management services for the inpatient and outpatient components of a specialty service line, such as cardiac, oncology, or orthopedics. The arrangement provides for and rewards physician engagement and leadership in a broad spectrum of activities that improve patient care and outcomes, generate cost efficiencies, and make the clinical service more competitive in the market.

With this approach, physicians have more clinical and operational influence than they have had traditionally, and the hospital gains from quality, safety, cost efficiency, and patient satisfaction improvements.

Changes necessitate new approaches to service line management

The healthcare industry will see many changes over the next five to 10 years as major tenets of healthcare reform legislation are enacted. Front and center will likely be the transition to value-based reimbursement models, such as bundled payments for episodes of care. New approaches to accountable service line management, which today are largely acute care–focused, may emerge as hospitals and physicians encounter the challenges of managing risks for utilization, outcomes, and defined payments. Preventive care, chronic disease management, and home care services are likely to be part of future service line portfolios.

Service line administrators and marketers planning for the future should identify and address elements that will change the requirements for success. The answers will provide the foundation for strategic decision-making regarding service line strategy, structure, and marketing investments. Key questions to raise and deliberate include the following:

- How will changes in policy and reimbursement shape future demand for the service line's services, and how will they affect financial performance?

- What will be the key levers of profitability and where does the service line stand in relationship to those requirements?
- How will the service line build and achieve distinct competencies in accountable clinical management?
- What needs and changes offer the best opportunity for profitable growth? Where are opportunities for service and/or market expansion? What new models of care should be considered?
- What is the future relationship of physicians to the service line? What mechanisms exist to align physician and service line interests? How do these opportunities vary by primary care versus subspecialists?
- What are the future opportunities for development and/or integration of physician, ambulatory, post acute, rehabilitation, and retail health services in the service line management model?
- What competitive strategies are likely to develop among and between healthcare providers in the market? When and how should the hospital cooperate, affiliate, or compete aggressively against current and new market entrants?
- What are the technological, facility, human resource, and capital investments required to support future growth and development in key service lines? What capabilities, systems, products, competitive positioning, marketing, and pricing strategies will be required?
- What guiding principles will best focus future strategy, structure, business and clinical initiatives, and investments?

Service Line Marketing Opportunities and Challenges

Marketing is an essential business discipline charged with creating profitable exchange relationships. Effective marketing starts with recognizing customers' needs and employs a mix of strategies configured to deliver distinct solutions to meet those needs. It is less about sales and promotion—although those are critical tools of marketing—and more about value creation through an orchestrated approach to creating markets, cultivating customers, delivering benefits, and building loyalty and repeat business.

Early service line marketing endeavors failed to deliver return on investments largely because promotional efforts were undertaken without an understanding of customers' needs or the complex selection and purchasing decision processes for health services. Marketers ran ads but didn't have responsibility for orchestrating the channel relationships (e.g., with physicians) that brought patients to the hospital. They printed brochures but didn't have influence in the design and configuration of clinical programs and processes that drive patient experience.

Concepts of segmentation, differentiation, customer experience, and value innovation took a while to emerge in health services marketing. Today, there is much greater recognition that successful service line marketing requires a partnership among clinical service line leaders and marketing professionals to discover market opportunities, target valued customer segments, cultivate enduring physician relationships, bring distinct programs to market, deliver against patient expectations, build a loyal customer base, and achieve the desired financial and strategic benefits. A common misconception of competition is that success is achieved by being better than the competition when, in fact, sustainable competitive advantage comes from being different from the competition by delivering a distinct but customer-relevant value proposition.

Summary

In many ways, service line marketing leaders have never had a more opportune time to better establish the discipline of marketing as a strategy-critical business competency. The underlying basis for competition in the industry is shifting, driven by the converging forces of healthcare reform, physician services restructuring, provider consolidations, consumer expectations, and networked information technologies. Changing economics are at the forefront, and make a compelling case for the role that marketers must play in an increasingly complex, competitive industry.

The opportunities to raise the bar in service line marketing are three-fold:

- First, to build a service line marketing approach that is strategic and focused on near-term growth, as well as creation of future customers, products, and channels
- Second, to establish the critical relationships and links across the value chain—clinical operations, finance, purchasing, IT, physicians, partnerships—and orchestrate alignment of customer needs and service line growth goals

- And third, to develop a results-oriented service line marketing function that delivers on revenue growth and profit goals

To take advantage of all these opportunities, marketers must adopt a profit-and-loss mind-set, transition from promotions-oriented tactics to growth-oriented strategic leadership, drive value innovation, and promote customer-centered practices.

References

Corrigan, Karen. "The CMO's Leadership Imperative." *Healthcare Strategy Alert,* Issue 3, 2010.

Davis, Scott M. *The Shift: The Transformation of Today's Marketers into Tomorrow's Growth Leaders.* Jossey-Bass, 2009.

Gee, Preston E. *Service Line Execution 2.0: Advanced Strategies for Progressive Hospitals.* HCPro, Inc., 2008.

Gee, Preston E. *Service Line Success: Eight Essential Rules.* ACHE, 2004.

Rebsaman, C.B.; Schad, Rachael; Corrigan, Karen. "Clinical Co-Management: Driving Service Line Success through Shared Leadership." Navvis & Company, April 2010.

CHAPTER 2

Creating a Strategic Marketing Framework

When developing a strategic marketing plan for a service line or portfolio of service lines, it is imperative to consider the organization's overall strategy to better understand and discern the distinct role that key clinical programs play in supporting and achieving macro growth goals. It is difficult, if not impossible, to gain organizational support and engagement in service line marketing plans if they are not aligned to the health system's strategy and performance objectives.

Aligning Health System Strategy and Service Line Goals

A health system's strategic plan helps leaders focus on the most critical elements to balance long-term goals with achievement of short-term business objectives. It is the master plan that guides the direction of the company as a whole, establishes the foundation for major business initiatives and investments, and builds commitment to the actions and resources required for success.

The key elements addressed in a hospital or health system strategic plan are:

- ***Competitive environment.*** The environmental assessment helps leaders understand the opportunities, competitive challenges, and future requirements of the market where the facility chooses to operate. It is imperative to the development of effective competitive strategy.
- ***Business definition.*** The corporate-level strategic plan also defines the boundaries of a health system's business model in terms of the company's mission, markets to be served, and structure.
- ***Strategic vision.*** A strategic vision is the guiding theme that articulates a health system's intentions for the future and states its aspirations for what it can and should become. The strategic vision is further defined by a set of goals and imperatives that establish long-term priorities and provide the framework for related activities, including marketing.
- ***Competitive advantage.*** A central role of strategy-making is to establish a positioning theme and formulate strategies that will differentiate an organization from its competition in ways that are meaningful to customers. Usually, this is achieved through a combination of program innovation, quality improvement, service excellence, strategic partnerships, or other business initiatives.
- ***Portfolio management.*** The system-level strategic plan also defines growth objectives, product offerings, and a selection of arenas in which the facility will compete. This includes decisions to expand current service line offerings, extend clinical programs into new geographic markets, or develop new clinical service lines or offerings, as well as to curtail investments in or divest underperforming business units.

- ***Organizational transformation.*** Last, the strategic plan addresses the organization's leadership structure, operating model, and internal culture. It also considers strategic relationships, capabilities, and investments that will be required for successful execution of the plan.

Service Line Business Planning Focuses Marketing Investments

Business planning at the service line level establishes growth, volume, and revenue goals and provides a more detailed approach to decision-making about which programs and services will be offered and to which audiences. Service line business plans address the actions and investments required to develop new services, acquire technology, add new facilities or equipment, build critical physician relationships, and define staffing needs, expertise, and other core competencies and capabilities.

In hospitals, business planning at the service line level is usually aimed at internal stakeholders. The business plan provides a formal statement of service line goals and objectives, the rationale for why they are believed attainable, and the plan for reaching those goals. While most business plans typically focus on financial goals, such as volume growth and profitability, service line plans also tend to address clinical matters, such as quality and safety improvements. This will probably increase in practice as outcomes are tied more directly to reimbursement.

Business plans are decision-making tools—showing what to focus on, how much to invest, and how to achieve targeted performance goals. The planning process should engage and draw on the knowledge of experts from finance, supply chain, human resources, IT, medical practice, and marketing, among others.

Marketing planning is an integral process of business planning. The service line manager and the marketing professional must collaborate to align service line priorities and marketing investments in order to achieve organizational goals and objectives. The business and marketing planning processes should provide additional analysis of the business environment and identification of market opportunities. They also should establish specific growth and revenue goals, select target markets and segments, and design a marketing strategy to reach, attract, and influence customers to use the organization's services.

The relationship between strategic planning, business planning, and marketing planning is illustrated in Figure 2.1.

FIGURE 2.1 ALIGNMENT OF STRATEGIC, BUSINESS, AND MARKETING PLANNING

	STRATEGIC PLANNING	BUSINESS PLANNING	MARKETING PLANNING
ROLE	To establish vision, strategic goals, and initiatives to improve the health system's long-term competitive performance	To develop plans and initiatives to activate the organization's strategy, allocate resource investments, and achieve growth objectives	To develop and administer marketing plans, programs, and activities that drive demand for the organization's branded service lines and products
FUNCTION	• Industry trends and forecasts • Long-range planning • Portfolio optimization • Strategic partnerships and alliances • Strategic investments • Strategic management	• SBU and service line planning • Operational and functional planning • Business modeling • Feasibilities and pro formas • Market and product expansion; mergers and acquisitions	• Market research • Service line marketing planning • Brand development and management • Product strategies • Advertising and promotions • Sales and distribution management
OUTPUTS	• Strategic vision • Organizational goals • Strategic priorities • Product portfolio strategies • Market expansion strategies **Inputs** →	• Role and scope • Growth and profitability goals • Service line priorities • Competitive capabilities • Operations **Inputs** →	• Brand vision and strategy • Marketing goals and plans • Product development • Advertising and promotions • Sales plans and strategies

Source: Navvis & Company

Marketing as Strategy: Markets, Products, and Channels

Marketing strategy focuses the organization's energies and resources on a course of action that leads to increased volumes, better profitability, and command of targeted growth opportunities. For most hospitals and health systems, service line marketing strategies are considered at two levels:

- ***Portfolio optimization.*** At the corporate level, decisions are made as to which of the many clinical offerings provide the best opportunity for growth, profitability, and improved competitive position. The objective is to optimize overall organizational performance through targeted activities and investments. Health systems cannot effectively focus marketing resources on every single service and, in fact, often suboptimize performance by trying to spread marketing dollars too thinly across too many programs.
- ***Service line optimization.*** Once service lines have been prioritized, then decisions should be made as to the marketing strategies that will be most effective in driving growth, improving financial performance, and developing a distinct market position for each of the select clinical programs.

Marketing strategy determines the choice of target segments or markets, the optimal mix and design of products and services to attract and build business from those segments, and the methods, structures, and relationships to channel partners—primarily physicians—who influence consumer choice for healthcare services. These are discussions and decisions that should be made with full agreement and support between marketing and the service line leader, chief financial officer, clinical program experts, and other key stakeholders.

The strategy is then translated into a service line marketing plan that integrates the health system's service line priorities, marketing goals, tactical actions, and marketing investments into a cohesive whole. The plan should contain a well-thought-out set of specific tactics to successfully implement the marketing strategy—for example, "Establish a rapid-access entry point of care to attract consumers seeking relief from acute onset of symptoms."

Marketing strategy isn't about media mix, screening events, or sales plans—these are tactical examples of planned activities that work together to achieve the strategy. Without a solid strategic foundation upon which to pin tactics and investments, marketing expenditures appear arbitrary and often lack support from internal stakeholders.

Positioning and differentiation: Creating sources of advantage

At the strategy-making level, two additional decisions should be made to focus service line marketing investments:

- How will the service line be positioned vis-à-vis the choices that target customers have for accessing care in the market?
- What programs, technologies, clinical expertise, customer service policies, physician relationships, and other aspects of our program provide true, distinctive benefits and points of differentiation between our service line and that of competitor organizations?

Service Line Brand Management

The mantra for health systems seeking leverage from service line marketing investments is simple: *Build the brand. Build the business.*

Brand management is fundamental to a successful service line growth strategy. This requires an explicit strategy and plan of action to position service lines, differentiate services, increase brand equity, and evolve service line brands in lockstep with the organization's overall brand strategy and business objectives. This also requires an alignment between service line operations and marketing that does not exist in many health systems. All too often, this creates a disconnect between what marketing promotes and what customers experience; closing the gap is paramount to building brand equity.

Brand is the totality of customer experience resulting from organizational decisions about positioning, design, development, and delivery of products and services. For far too long, health systems have been trying to build brands almost exclusively through communications processes, which waste marketing dollars and undermine competitive performance when the image portrayed is not the experience delivered. Powerful service line brands do not happen by accident. They are carefully discerned, purposefully positioned, and aggressively managed to create connections that stimulate demand, build customer loyalty, drive growth, and improve profitability.

The gap between investments in service line brand building and realized return cannot be closed with brand advertising alone—nor can it be resolved by customer service, clinical quality, lean operations, and other initiatives pursued in isolation of a comprehensive, integrated approach to better leverage outcomes for market advantage. The only way to narrow the brand equity gap is to effect strategic, operational, clinical, physician, and marketing alignment at the service line level to create and deliver a meaningful, differentiated, and durable brand value proposition. Brand alignment builds the brand-driven culture that transforms a service line—and an organization—from one that simply "promotes a brand" to one that "delivers the brand."

Five key areas of brand management should be addressed in the service line marketing strategy:

1. Determine the service line's unique **brand value proposition**. How you plan to create and deliver value to current and prospective customers is fundamental to long-term success. What significant customer-centered benefits (e.g., more timely appointments, better coordinated care, personalized service, best-in-class physician talent, faster pain relief) will your patients gain as a result of choosing your hospital?

2. Agree on service line **brand identity**. Names may be about egos, but brands are about business. The right brand identity should, first and foremost, ease the selection process for your customers. Brand identity for the service line should be chosen in the context of the health system's overall brand strategy.

3. Create **brand alignment** across operating, clinical, and marketing systems, and build a discipline to channel investments into those things

that matter most. If your core positioning is about highly personalized patient care, then systems must be aligned to make that happen for every patient, every day.

4. Hardwire customer service, operating, and patient care processes to deliver on the brand. Patient experience is born through **brand activation**, a process whereby the brand value proposition is translated and transformed into actionable principles, features, service standards, and behaviors. Remember that brand reputation is built primarily through customer experience.

5. Enhance **brand performance**. Establish and monitor key metrics regarding growth, revenue, profitability, brand awareness, brand preference, customer advocacy, and staff engagement. Identify growth opportunities in key segments, markets, and channels. Address barriers that may limit the power of your brand to move market share.

Prioritizing Marketing Resource Allocations

Marketing executives must carefully prioritize and allocate their limited marketing resources to those service lines and service line marketing initiatives that have the best potential for return on marketing investments. Within that construct, there are two levels for consideration:

- Which service lines offer the best opportunity for growth and profitability?

- Within priority service lines, what initiatives will best achieve marketing goals?

Executives must determine what service lines to invest in for growth and what activities contribute most to those growth objectives. Both top-down and bottom-up approaches to resource allocation are necessary for success. Top down approaches are needed for strategic planning across the system's portfolio of service lines; bottom up approaches help develop individual marketing budgets within the service line.

Top down considerations are derived from the analysis of the following key elements:

- Overall utilization, volume, and demand projections
- Rate of market growth for encounters and procedures
- Reimbursement and profitability rates and trends
- Organizational capacity for new growth
- Physician supply, access, capacity, and alignment
- Health system competencies, technologies, and facilities
- Patient experience and satisfaction
- Quality indicators and rankings
- Competitive positioning, brand strength, and market distinctiveness

By comparing this information across all service lines, it soon becomes evident that a focused subset should be targeted. Many organizations rank their service lines and clinical programs in order to determine the level of marketing investment allocated to each. For example:

- Top tier service lines are those with the most potential for growth, contribution to profitability, and brand distinctiveness. These service lines would receive the majority of marketing investment.
- Second tier service lines are those with modest growth potential and positive contribution margins. A minority of marketing resources would be invested here.
- Third tier service lines are those critical to the mission, but are not growing or unprofitable, or they are underperforming in some significant way. These service lines receive minimal, if any, marketing investments and should be evaluated for ongoing viability.

A hospital may determine, for example, that it will invest 60% of total marketing resources in Tier One service lines; 30% in Tier Two; and 10% to maintain minimal support of Tier Three service lines. These percentages can be manipulated, but they should provide enough investment in the most important growth areas to produce results.

Once the decision of which service lines to grow has been made, then marketing planning should serve to guide how resources are allocated against the marketing mix for top tier clinical programs—strategic decisions should clearly guide this. Just because television advertising costs more to produce doesn't mean it should be allocated more resources—especially if marketing demand is not influenced by mass media.

The following are investment considerations that come into play:

- Research and development to build, expand, and enhance the mix of service offerings
- Program development and patient care experience design
- Building brand awareness and stimulating demand in target customer segments
- Cultivating and strengthening access channels, physician relations, and referrals
- Sales, third party contracting, and pricing
- Advertising, promotions, marketing events, and co-marketing partnerships
- Marketing infrastructure and customer relations management systems (e.g. CRM systems, call centers, online referrals and registrations, tracking and reporting, etc.)

The secret to success in marketing resource allocation is to know where investments return the biggest bang. Consumer influenced or directed services such as bariatric surgery, plastic surgery, or sports marketing require more investment in direct consumer marketing, events marketing, and call center support. Whereas, marketing for services and procedures influenced more by physician referrals should be more heavily invested in sales, physician relations, and new clinical program development.

Invest strategically to build competitive advantage

Traditionally, healthcare institutions have allocated marketing resources based on the most profitable service lines focused on short-term results. The problem with taking this approach alone is that it leads to sub-optimization of assets, with investment decisions that can lose value over time (e.g., while investing marketing resources to protect current market share, the hospital overlooks growth opportunities). With a longer-term outlook, marketing resource allocation decisions should consider the entire service line portfolio, while smartly focusing investments on critical performance drivers.

Service line marketers can do that by viewing resource allocation from the consumer perspective in addition to the service line perspective. Then, they should target strategic customer segments based on growth potential by understanding what those customers want, how they behave, and how to influence choices. While the traditional approach has been to focus marketing resources on the "best" customers, new thinking suggests that organizations should also allocate resources to micro-targets of consumers to predict and influence behavior. This will become more important from a community health perspective, as providers begin to be reimbursed based on health outcomes from the entire episode of care.

Marketing allocation challenges can be addressed in three steps:

1. Identifying and targeting high value segments—those most likely to drive volume and profitability
2. Conducting marketing experiments to model, understand, analyze, and predict how different marketing actions will affect consumer behavior

3. Using the results to determine the best continued actions and investments for marketing effectiveness

One way to reinforce strategic focus of resource allocation is to categorize service offerings into different buckets, such as the tiers described above. For example, Tier One could be labeled "growth," Tier Two "protect and defend," and Tier Three "beyond scope." Budgeting resources are easier when marketers can focus on what to protect and defend, allow to sunset, or invest to grow.

Once the priority service lines have been identified, optimize marketing resources across those sectors with a plan to measure and communicate the effectiveness of resources allocated.

Setting priorities

Strategic resource allocation to support service line brands is complex. Smart investments will require the willingness to think long-term, hire analytical support, and use new media tools that support the service line strategy.
Every marketer should take the following steps:

- Make strategic allocation decisions based on future value, not historical growth—this helps identify growth segments.
- Once allocation of service line marketing resources has been determined overall (top-down), then focus on marketing budgets within each service line category (bottom-up).
- Make sure each service line's marketing budget plan has specific, measurable objectives (e.g., increase emergency department patient capture by two points or increase immunization rates by 20%).

- Use pilot projects to determine spending effectiveness. Test to see whether increased or reduced spending has had an impact on consumer behavior, which will lead to an effective budgeting process.

Marketers Held to a Higher Standard

Marketers face myriad dilemmas regarding resource allocation. They need to evaluate whether such resources are used wisely and whether traditional methods of resource allocation are still effective in today's marketing and healthcare environment.

In addition, today's healthcare marketing team faces challenges on several fronts:

- Restricted budgets
- Demand for analytic benchmarks
- Rise of new media

While dealing with budget constraints, marketing departments are under increasing pressure to demonstrate return on investment for marketing dollars spent. Meanwhile, with the rise of new media, marketers are facing highly fragmented media outlets and micro-targeted consumer segments. The good news is that there are tools to monitor every step of consumer behavior, which will help decision-makers understand the value of customer investments (see Figure 2.2 for resource allocation models). The challenge lies in the need to develop analytical expertise as the marketing discipline evolves—and translate that into measurable objectives.

FIGURE 2.2

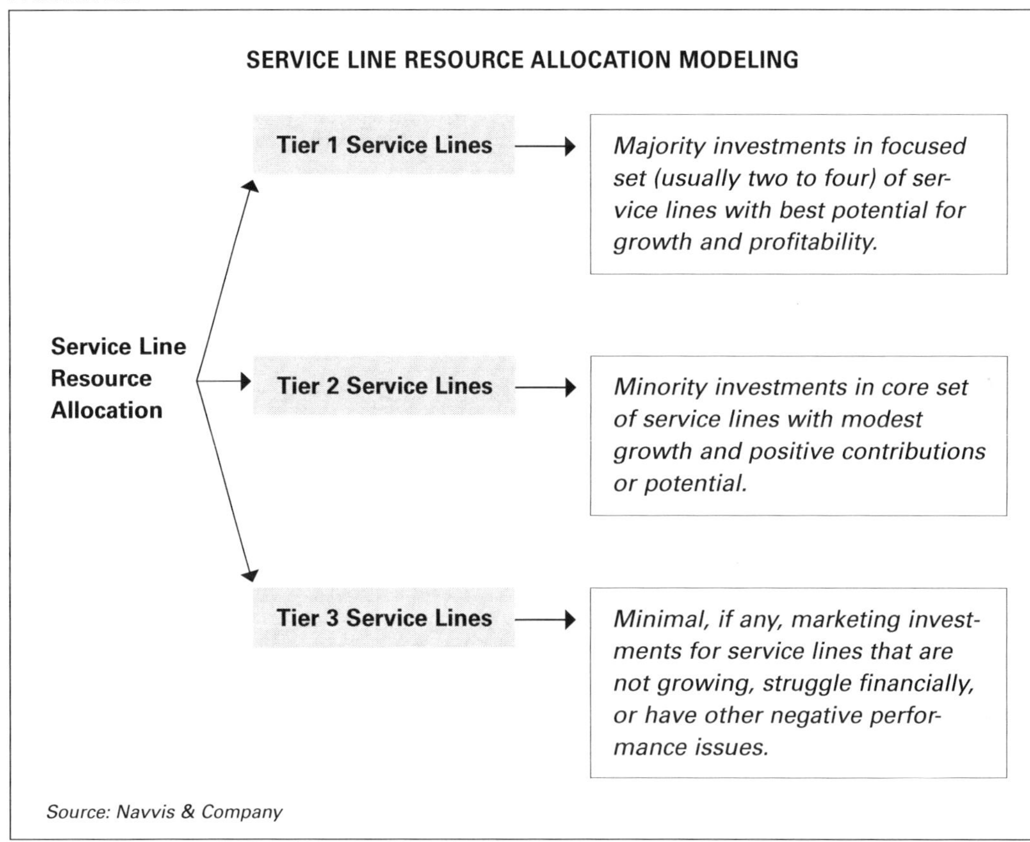

Source: Navvis & Company

Summary

Successful service line marketing begins with the development of an overall strategic marketing framework aligned to health system strategy, growth, and business objectives. Marketers and service line administrators should work collaboratively through business and marketing planning processes to focus on those opportunities with the greatest potential for return on investment. This requires decisions about which service lines will be prioritized for marketing investments and what marketing activities will best produce desired growth, profitability, and customer loyalty. Critical choices about markets, products, and channels are the foundation to create the positioning, differentiation, and brand strategies that stimulate and drive customer preference, selection, and purchase.

References

Aaker, David A. *Building Strong Brands.* The Free Press,1996.

Athmann-King, Corrigan and Gelineau. *Impact Marketing: Optimizing Value and Return on Investment.* Society for Healthcare Strategy and Market Development, 2004.

Davis, Scott M. *Brand Asset Management: Driving Profitable Growth through Your Brands.* Jossey-Bass, 2002.

Day, George. *Market Driven Strategy: Processes for Creating Value.* Free Press, 1999.

Goldman, Ellen F. *Results-Oriented Strategic Planning.* Society for Healthcare Strategy and Market Development, 2002.

Keller, Kevin. *Strategic Brand Management.* Prentice Hall, Inc., 1998.

Kotler, Philip; Keller, Kevin. *Marketing Management,* 13th Edition. Prentice-Hall, Inc., 2008.

CHAPTER 3

Marketing Planning, Processes, and Tools

Service line marketing planning is basically the process of identifying growth opportunities, crafting strategies to pursue those opportunities, and determining specific tactics and investments to achieve results. Marketing planning requires a careful examination of all relevant strategic issues, including macro-environmental industry trends, the markets served by the service line, physicians, competitors, organizational capabilities, and changing consumer needs.

Market Intelligence: Insights and Discovery

The starting point for developing an effective service line marketing strategy is gathering meaningful customer, market, organizational, competitive, and brand information that is not simply a history of what has been and a snapshot of what is, but also serves as a tool to accurately and opportunistically forecast emerging needs and opportunities.

Advanced research and analytic techniques are the basis for sound decision-making on positioning, segmentation, targeting, product design, channel strategies, pricing, and promotion. It helps an organization identify customers' choices for accessing care in the market and whether they are hospital-, physician-, or insurance plan–centric in their decision-making. Profiling key customer segments helps determine needs and brand preferences, as well as what influence emotional commitment and market barriers have on choice and loyalty. Without such metrics, organizations cannot identify market strengths and opportunities in key geographic, payer, and referral channels.

Unfortunately, many hospitals underinvest in meaningful customer, market, and competitive diagnostics, which differ substantially from the typical consumer awareness and preference research so prevalent in the industry. A properly facilitated market intelligence process lays the foundation for all future stages of building a powerful service line brand and growth strategy. From data to insights to strategy, market intelligence reveals opportunities and identifies how channels, competition, and company practices drive brand performance. It informs positioning, segmentation, targeting, product design, service delivery, pricing, and promotional decision-making, and, in the process, creates the means for building ongoing relationships with customers.

Most important, market analysis provides the primary foundation for evaluating, projecting, and measuring the impact and effectiveness of marketing strategy on service line performance.

Marketing analysis is typically structured in a few key domains: market, customer, competitor, and company analysis.

Market analysis

Creating an overall profile of the market is important to building an understanding of the macro-level industry trends and local dynamics most likely to influence demand, growth, and profitability of clinical service lines. Service line market analysis should consider, among other factors:

- Health industry trends and forecasting, such as healthcare policy, economics, sociodemographics, industry structure, and labor supply
- Service line–specific trends and forecasting, such as advances in technology, changes in clinical practice, changes in payment and reimbursement methodologies, and disease incidence and utilization trends
- Demand analysis and projections for both inpatient and outpatient services
- Physician supply, demand, alignment, and referral patterns
- Changes in demographic patterns, geographic density, and population shifts

Customer analysis

Customer analysis is critical to understanding consumer needs, behaviors, purchasing patterns, decision drivers, and other factors that influence utilization, satisfaction, and loyalty. It also provides information to support segmentation and targeting, which is discussed in greater detail in the next section. An effective customer assessment includes:

- Current and projected prevalence and incidence of disease and contributing risk factors

- Customer perceptions, attitudes, selections, and purchasing behaviors regarding healthcare services
- Brand awareness, preference, and customer loyalty
- Segmentation analysis, including customer information that is organized into meaningful target markets

Competitor analysis

Competitor analysis is central to understanding the strengths and weaknesses of the service line in the context of local market competition. Service line marketers should consider the brand power of its competitors, strengths and weaknesses of clinical programs, market coverage and access issues, and physician referral patterns in terms of recommending one institution over another. Marketers should also be cognizant that competition may not always come from other hospital service lines, but can present from retail ventures, physician ventures, niche ambulatory players, or even from pharma or biotech firms that provide substitute solutions for care delivered by hospitals.

A competitor analysis should cover the following:

- Market structure and competitive activity, including the number and types of competition for service line offerings, new market entrants, acquisitions or strategic alliances, and physician alignment patterns
- Market position, strategies, strengths, and weaknesses of competitors
- Trended volume, market share, and financial performance of competitor service lines
- New models of care, emerging technologies, and disruptive innovations

Company analysis

Company analysis helps service line leaders and marketers understand the service line's core competencies and distinct sources of competitive advantage or disadvantage, as well as its cost position, quality performance, and customer satisfaction position. It's a principal process for identifying how administrative and clinical operations must be configured, managed, and delivered to optimize marketing investment. Key aspects of company analysis will include:

- Important information and metrics regarding overall service line financial and operational performance
- Analysis of the major diagnosis-related groups, services, procedures, and offerings from the service line, identifying the scope, scale, contributions, and potential of each
- Assessment of core competencies, capabilities, capacity, technologies, and other programmatic elements central to overall business performance

There are many ways to collect and analyze data; the key to success is determining those marketing factors that best support service line marketers in discovering and understanding key opportunities and issues that will need to be addressed and resolved through the service line marketing planning process. An effective marketing intelligence system typically relies on both internal and external data sources, and also on primary and secondary research.

Segmentation and Targeting

Segmentation and targeting are key concepts to enable positioning and differentiation strategies. Segmentation is the process whereby you identify and size customer groups with similar needs, motivations, values, and behaviors, and targeting is where you choose to focus upon those segments that have the greatest potential to drive growth and profitability.

These processes are essential to customizing strategies that differentiate your service line and produce an optimal return on marketing investment.

Defining market opportunities

The concept of market segmentation embodies the idea that no single product or service, or single approach to delivering a service or product, can meet the needs of or satisfy all customers. Accordingly, segmentation can identify specific growth opportunities with a large heterogeneous market by identifying groups of consumers with similar needs or like characteristics that can be reached through a marketing strategy tailored to target consumers' preferences and behaviors.

Segmentation is both a science and an art; market segments are identified by applying combinations of variables such as geography, gender, income, disease state, and other factors to subdivide a market, and opportunities are discovered by inventive combinations of those variables that provide unique insights into customer needs.

There are an endless number of variables that can be applied. In healthcare, the categories detailed in the following sections are the most relevant bases for segmentation.

Geographic segmentation

This category addresses service line marketing opportunities or challenges in specific communities or regions. The objective of geographic segmentation is to discover the similarities or differences in customer needs and preferences to support highly targeted marketing strategies. For example, a region or community with a much higher concentration of older adults is a more favorable target for cardiovascular services than an area with young singles or families.

Levels of market penetration by community or region provide another way to look at an organization's strategy for those different areas. If a hospital is highly penetrated—has high market share—in a specific geographic area, then its strategy for that area is defensive: How do we maintain our favorable position? Conversely, if a health system wants to establish a position in an area where it is not currently pulling a lot of volume, its strategy will need to be an offensive one: What must we do to capture market share from our competitors?

Geographic segmentation also provides insights into how consumers may be clustered by income and lifestyle similarities or differences, and into behavioral considerations such as convenience and access.

Demographic segmentation

This segment considers characteristics such as gender, age, race, ethnicity, and life stage, and the implications of those variables on healthcare needs, preferences, and purchasing behaviors. Demographic variables are used more frequently by service line marketers than many other factors, as they are easier to measure and associate with specific healthcare needs. For example, the healthcare industry targets women over the age of 40 for mammography and men over the age of 50 for regular prostate exams, young women and families use more OB/GYN and pediatric services, African American men are at greater risk for heart disease and stroke, and frail elders are at risk for fractures.

While demographic variables provide a valuable, highly measurable, and predictable method of market segmentation, demographics alone won't produce enough data to help service line leaders understand how to move market share. That requires multiple levels of analysis and segmentation using some of the variables described in the following sections.

Socioeconomic segmentation

This category considers characteristics such as household income, education level, and lifestyle. This method of segmentation is popular with companies that develop different products or offerings at different price points. Automobile manufacturers, for example, may have both economy and luxury cars in their portfolios.

The "luxury" segment equivalent in healthcare is often associated with cosmetic surgery, concierge medicine, executive physicals, vision-correction surgery, and other services not typically covered by health plans. However, service line leaders can appeal to this segment through positioning, facility design, amenity, and customer care strategies. Cosmetic and laser eye surgery practices broaden their universe of customers beyond the small numbers typically comprising the luxury segment by offering financing for procedures.

Most healthcare marketing plans consider the health insurance status of their customer base as a means of segmentation and targeting to optimize profitability. It's important to understand the contribution margin of various insured segments to focus growth strategies.

Psychographic segmentation

This segment divides consumers into groups based upon variables such as attitudes and tastes. It assumes, for example, that not all people in a certain demographic segment have the same needs, wants, or preferences. One of the more common marketing mistakes made by healthcare marketers is failing to consider the psychographic differences in generational cohorts. Not all baby boomers are demanding, proactive healthcare consumers; not all seniors are doctor-dependent.

A recent segmentation study looked at older women (a demographic segment) with heart disease (an epidemiologic needs-based segment) and discovered two distinct psychographic subsegments: risk-aware women and risk-naïve women. The importance of this finding is recognizing that the same marketing strategy will not attract, serve, or satisfy both segments. Different approaches must be devised to effectively penetrate both.

Behavioral segmentation

This group looks for patterns of actions in defined circumstances. One method of behavioral segmentation is identifying occasions when certain needs occur. Sales of flowers, for example, are higher on occasions such as Valentine's Day or anniversaries. In healthcare, individuals traveling to developing countries may need immunizations that would not be done as a matter of routine healthcare. Parents anticipating the birth of a new baby need to find a pediatrician. Leveraging occasions such as breast cancer awareness month may stimulate demand for mammography. The beginning of every school year creates a spike in sports physicals. Another example is a hospital that offers a fracture and stress evaluation clinic on Saturday mornings following Friday evening high-school sports events.

Usage rates (e.g., high, medium or low users) are another factor often considered in behavioral segmentation, as are benefits sought. Retail care clinics located in grocery, pharmacy, or department store chains provide the primary benefit of convenient access for consumers with minor illnesses.

Epidemiologic needs-based segmentation

This segment employs variables such as incidence, cause, and prevalence of disease to size and target markets. There is no doubt that in this industry epidemiologic segmentation is the first step in market opportunity analysis for service line leaders. Service line strategies focusing on cardiovascular, oncology, orthopedic, or neurology patients can be further segmented into specific disease states/stages of illness. It is not sufficient to target the universe of women as a preferred segment for a women's cardiovascular program—the segment must be better and more narrowly defined as women *with or at risk for* heart disease to increase diagnostic, treatment, and procedural volumes. Even then, women with or at risk for heart disease can be further subsegmented into needs-based groups for target marketing.

There are many other variables in addition to those described above—see Figure 3.1 for examples of the primary variables in healthcare. Service line marketers should also look at the audiences they serve in unique ways. A multivariable approach often reveals new opportunities to differentiate your service line offerings.

FIGURE 3.1

EXAMPLES OF SEGMENTATION VARIABLES

Geographic	Demographic	Life Stage	Health Attitude	Disease/Condition
• Primary • Secondary • Tertiary	• Age • Sex • Race and ethnicity • Generational cohort • Education/ income	• Mid-life transition • Active empty nester • Nearing retirement • Adult caregivers • Active moms	• Health competent • Health worried • Health dependent • Indifferent	General wellness Episodic issues Chronic disease

Source: Navvis & Company

For example, segmentation can identify and size available consumer segments for your service line, identify unmet needs that can lead to approaching the market in new and innovative ways, and reveal which segments offer the greatest volume, revenue, profit, and strategic fit. See Figure 3.2 for an example of needs-based segments.

FIGURE 3.2

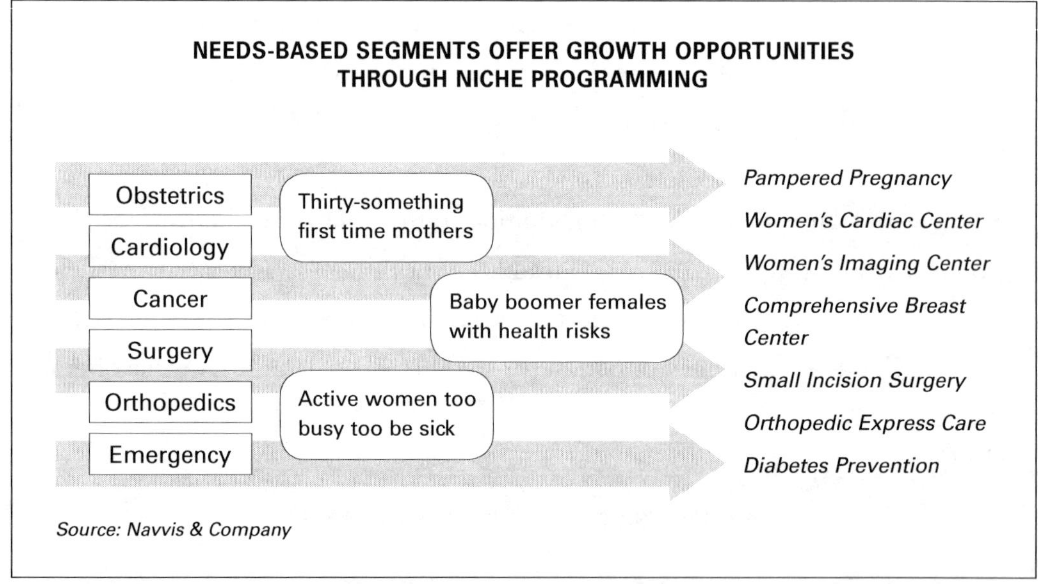

Source: Navvis & Company

Targeting customers: Choosing growth markets

Service line marketers should continue to find unique ways to look at the audiences they serve. A multivariable approach often reveals new opportunities to differentiate your service line offerings.

Segmentation can identify and size available consumer segments for your service line, highlight unmet needs that can lead you to approach the market in new and innovative ways, and reveal which segments offer the greatest volume, revenue, profit, and strategic fit.

Targeting is the strategy of selecting which market segments to serve. Many healthcare organizations choose to pursue a mass marketing approach whereupon service lines are configured, positioned, and promoted to the broadest number of possible consumers, but others focus marketing efforts on one to three key segments with the potential to positively influence sales and profitability.

Marketers that pursue **mass or undifferentiated marketing strategies** defend its cost, as less customization of the marketing mix is required to appeal to different segments. This strategy can be effective for health systems that hold a dominant brand position for given service lines and where the additional investments required to serve distinct segments is unlikely to benefit sales and profitability. Hospitals with strong cardiovascular or maternity brands, for example, often practice mass marketing initiatives to reach the broadest possible customer group.

Marketers that pursue **target or differentiated marketing** for service lines have identified multiple—usually two to three—segments where there is greater opportunity to drive volume growth and achieve a stronger competitive position. This is particularly effective in those markets where health system or service brands are highly commoditized, or where hospitals challenge competitors that hold dominant positions. Organizations that choose this approach must recognize that this strategy requires additional investment, both in operations and in marketing, to create, deliver, and promote services to different customer segments. For example, many orthopedic service line marketers employ differentiated strategies to reach distinct, high-impact, needs-based targets, such as athletes with sports injuries or aging baby boomers for joint replacements. While most health systems generally seek to pursue mass marketing or at least two or three targeted high-impact segments to shape service line growth, a few focus on **niche or concentrated marketing**, where the objective is to become the preferred and dominant brand in a narrow but profitable market segment. Instead of going after a smaller share of a larger market, the marketer sees opportunity to garner larger share in select segments. This may be particularly useful where resources are limited or, again, where hospitals must challenge larger, entrenched competitors.

To be effective, this strategy requires considerable research, focused program design, flawless execution, and unwavering commitment to serving the needs of the niche segment better than anyone else in the market. Niche strategies may include focused markets for a specific clinical, disease, or procedural focus, such as bariatric surgery, or around a particular customer type, such as people attracted to convenience care services.

Hospitals may choose different approaches to segmentation and targeting for different service lines. A marketer, for example, may opt to pursue a mass marketing or undifferentiated strategy for a health system's cardiac program, targeted tactics for its orthopedic program, and a niche strategy for general surgery. The method chosen should be the one that will best achieve service line growth and profitability goals. In any case, distinct criteria on which to base segmentation and targeting decisions should follow three general rules:

- The segment is **measurable.** To be able to project the volume and revenue potential of a market, you must be able to determine its size, usage patterns, and growth potential.
- The segment is **meaningful.** The segment should be large enough to have sufficient volume and growth potential.

- The segment is **marketable.** A marketable segment is one whose needs have been identified and can be reached and served by the hospital in an effective, efficient way.

Segments that meet these criteria provide the service line marketer with viable opportunities on which to focus marketing tactics and investments.

Competitive positioning

Positioning is a concept made popular in the early 1980s by Jack Trout and Al Ries in their book *Positioning: The Battle for Your Mind.* It involves the sum of marketing activities—from product design to customer service policies to pricing decisions to marketing communications messaging—that establishes differentiation for a brand, product, or service. While positioning is something you do, the actual position that you hold results from the aggregate perception of a market or target segment about your service line in relation to the competition.

When done well, positioning establishes a distinct reference point set in relation to the competition by focusing on one or more features, attributes, or benefits that are meaningful to target customer groups. Once a position is solidly established and "owned" by a particular brand, it is very difficult for others to claim the same point or points of distinction. This is particularly true when the positioning strategy evokes a strong emotional response or attachment to a brand. Psychological positioning like this has much greater sustainability than tactics focused on service line offerings or features that can be copied by competitors. For example, hospitals that offer 30 minute wait-time guarantees in the emergency room may have a competitive edge only until other hospitals replicate the service.

Positioning strategies are important for hospitals that focus on specific segments for service line growth (see Figure 3.3). A maternity service line trying to attract first-time mothers should position the OB program differently to that segment than if it were targeting older, high-risk moms. If both segments are considered high-impact targets, then program offerings, clinical expertise, physician specialists, and promotions strategies must come together to appeal to both markets (see Figure 3.4).

FIGURE 3.3

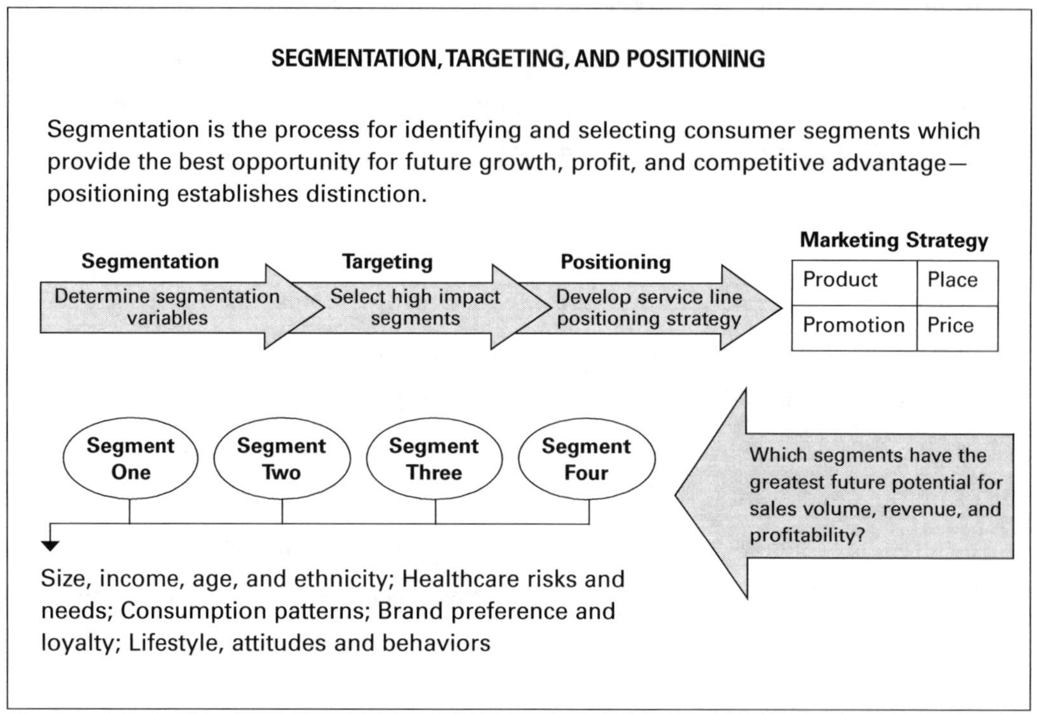

FIGURE 3.4

HIGH IMPACT SEGMENTS FOCUS BUSINESS, CLINICAL, AND MARKETING INITIATIVES

Segmentation serves to align and focus the service line's business development, clinical programming, brand building, and marketing efforts in order to achieve growth goals.

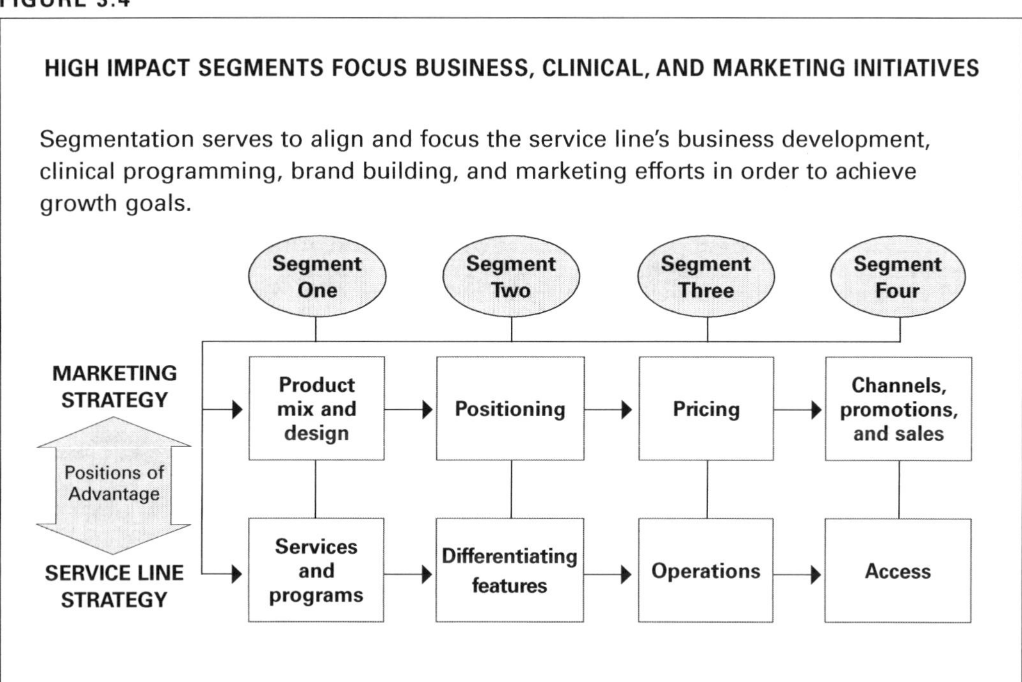

The Marketing Mix: Fundamental to Target Marketing

One of the first concepts taught in Marketing 101 is the marketing mix, otherwise known as the four Ps of marketing, which is symbolized by the equation:

Price ≤ Product + Place + Promotion

This equation encompasses all of the activities and tools available for developing and managing marketing action plans.

What does this equation represent? In order for a marketing strategy to be successful, the *value* of services received must be perceived to be greater than the price paid for a product or service. And value is embodied in the sum total of elements—positioning, product design, accessibility, customer service, clinical quality, convenience, brand, etc.—experienced or perceived by the customer. Organizations can manipulate any element of the equation to optimize marketing outcomes, such as sales growth, market penetration, or brand preference.

The dilemma faced by many healthcare marketers is that, historically, healthcare organizations have overinvested in the promotions end of the marketing mix at the expense of the other elements of the formula that create true customer value. And healthcare marketers will be the first to volunteer that this all too often results in underperformance for marketing investments.

Still, marketers often find themselves challenged to bring clinical operations, administrative functions, finance, and marketing people to the table to define and clarify the value proposition and to orchestrate activities across the value chain to bring a true, competitively differentiated service line offering to the market.

An effective service line marketing plan should address all aspects of the marketing mix, with particular emphasis on how that mix differs by target segment:

- ***Product strategies.*** In any business, revenue targets are achieved by selling products and services. Hence, the initial ingredient in the service line marketing mix is the product strategy aimed at target market segments. It includes the specific product or services being offered, but also extends the definition of the product by linking it with intangible services and experiences.

- ***Pricing strategies.*** Pricing presents an interesting dilemma to healthcare marketers because the prevailing reimbursement model shields many customers from the direct impact of the cost for services rendered. However, as consumers begin to bear a larger share of healthcare costs and as new retail models emerge, price becomes an increasingly important aspect of marketing management.
- ***Channel strategies.*** Healthcare marketers should develop channel strategies for all the intermediaries and relationships that connect a customer to the service line offerings. In most cases, the primary channel relationship is with physicians who refer or admit patients to the service line. Marketing intermediaries can also include employers, health plans, social agencies, and other providers, as well as direct access channels such as the ER or retail channels such as convenient care clinics. The marketing plan should carefully analyze how these intermediaries may or actually do influence consumer choice. It will then be possible to develop distinct strategies for cultivating relationships and increasing referrals.
- ***Promotion strategies.*** Promotions usually include a mix of advertising and personal selling strategies designed to build demand and sales for the service line. Advertising is generally used to create and sustain demand by building awareness of the company's products and services

and how they differ from those of competitors. Numerous advertising and promotional tools may be considered; the specific ones chosen for the mix should be selected and tested for maximum impact. Responses to a direct marketing effort may generate opportunities for personal selling. That tactic may also be part of an explicit, proactive approach to reach and influence consumers and marketing intermediaries.

Product design, development, and positioning

The term *product* when used in a marketing context is conceptual. A product is anything that can be offered to a customer in exchange, usually for money, in order to satisfy a need or want. It can include physical goods such as eyeglasses or contact lenses, or services such as eye examinations or vision correction surgery. In its broadest sense, *product* can also mean people (e.g., politicians, entertainers) or places (e.g., Bahamas, Disney World), and even events or ideas.

In service line marketing, *product* primarily refers to the core service provided to a customer or patient (e.g., joint replacement surgery, cardiac catheterization, or bariatric surgery). What makes the concept of product so complex, particularly in health services marketing, is that any one medical service or procedure is rarely experienced in isolation of other services. Someone having joint replacement surgery, for example, has several physician visits in advance of the surgery, perhaps with multiple physicians. He or she has x-rays and other diagnostic tests. Perhaps the patient goes to an informational class or participates in a "joint camp" program. After surgery, he or she may go to physical therapy or have in-home nursing support or rehab services. The patient may need prescription drugs to manage pain or require crutches or other types of medical equipment during recovery.

The actual product, therefore, from the marketer's point of view should be considered as the aggregate or bundle of activities and touchpoints that create the overall patient experience. Product or service design is a purposeful endeavor to create an experience that delivers on the core positioning strategy or value proposition. The key question for the service line marketer is: What combination of features and attributes delivers the core benefit sought by our target market? If a service line positions and promotes a minimally invasive surgery procedure around a core benefit of a quick return to normal life activities, how should pre-procedure, registration, discharge, and home recovery elements be designed to support that idea?

The concept of aggregating and marketing bundled services will become even more important in the future as payment reforms shift financial risk to providers for managing an episode of care across multiple parts of the care continuum. Service line design will need to consider not only those attributes that satisfy patient needs, but also how all the elements work together to achieve the utilization, quality, and cost requirements for profitability.

Product development and expansion within a service line structure are key elements of a growth strategy. New clinical capabilities and programs help retain current customers, extend service line offerings to additional customers, improve patient satisfaction, tap new sources of revenue, enhance clinical outcomes, and improve margins. Catalysts for product development may include acquisition of a new clinical technology, recruitment of specialists who do procedures not currently offered by the hospital, or discovery of a unique market segment opportunity. A robust product or service line development process will help bring new services to market faster and with greater potential for success.

Channel Strategies and Referral Relationships

Channel strategies address how customers are connected to a product or service. For most service lines, the primary channel relationship is with physicians who refer or admit patients to a product or service. Marketing intermediaries can also include employers, health insurers, social service agencies, and other healthcare providers, such as skilled nursing facilities. Emergency rooms can serve as strategic channels for key needs such as chest pain. Increasingly, consumers are turning to the Internet to connect to services and products. Hospitals are developing online referral tools and second-opinion programs and actively participating in social networking communities to reach and influence patients.

Marketers should assess how and what percentages of patient volumes come through which channels, as well as the attractiveness (in terms of profitability contributions) of different channels.

Physician supply, alignment, and engagement

Marketing success depends heavily upon the physician network that attracts, cares for, and refers patients to clinical services. The credentials, expertise, availability, and reputation of service line specialists can make or break a growth strategy. The relationship between specialists and the broader community of primary care and other physicians is critical to ensure an adequate flow of referrals. Clinical quality, patient satisfaction, cost efficiency, and practice advancements are contingent upon intensity of physician engagement.

Service line marketing plans should address several key questions: How many and what type of physicians are needed in what locations to produce desired service line volumes and revenues? What strategies should be pursued to attract, engage, and retain those physicians? How do we cultivate referrals to key specialists and clinical programs?

By quantifying current and projected demand for services and assessing the supply and location of current medical staff members, as well as area physicians who do not currently refer to the health system's service line, most marketers can get a clear picture of where deficits and opportunities exist in terms of physician coverage and referral patterns.

Across the United States, physician practices are undergoing massive change. Both primary care physician groups and subspecialists are joining health systems in tighter alignment structures ranging from employment to service line comanagement agreements to clinical joint ventures. In some markets, the private practice physician structure is alive and well; in others, it has dramatically diminished.

Service line marketing plans must consider the structure, supply, and nature of physician relationships. A comprehensive assessment of supply, need, and engagement strategies should be incorporated in the strategic marketing plan. The following five key methods are typically employed:

1. **Recruitment.** Recruitment strategies address physician shortages when supply-and-demand assessments indicate a need for additional physicians in a particular specialty or to support service line growth goals. Hospitals often try to support the recruitment efforts of existing practices; increasingly, however, hospitals are initiating recruitment to bring new practices to an area or for employment by the health system itself.

2. **Retention.** Top-producing physicians should be targeted for retention based upon historic commitment to activity in the service line for inpatient and outpatient service volumes. In addition to determining where coverage deficits exist, service line leaders need to give thoughtful consideration to marketplace realities. Is the organization vulnerable to losing current medical staff members? Are local competitors expanding their existing services—or adding new ones—for which they will need additional physician coverage? Retention is a strategy that usually arises when a hospital feels at risk of losing a loyal group of physicians.

3. **Redirection.** Physician candidates for redirection strategies are typically those aligned with competitor hospitals. Redirection is the process of finding, courting, and recruiting physicians who are not currently aligned with an institution. It often involves persuading physicians to

switch allegiance from one hospital to another. Organizations spend less time on redirection because it is a difficult strategy requiring lengthier negotiations, more resources, and greater effort. Redirecting physicians who are already loyal to another institution requires research, creativity, and a persuasive package based on marketplace intelligence. Before initiating a redirection, organizations should carefully develop the alignment package that will be presented to those doctors during initial discussions. If redirection candidates are unaligned and meet the organization's criteria, what will motivate those doctors to establish a new referral pattern?

4. **Redeployment.** The goal of redeployment is to increase practice volumes through a better geographic location for the practice or through the presence of multiple practice sites. Physicians usually maintain offices on or close to the hospital campus where they practice. But some service line leaders are now seeking to place doctors in outlying areas, where new or more desirable markets can be tapped.

5. **Retirement.** Transition planning should be considered for top-producing physicians over the age of 55. Like any business, medical practices have life cycles. Physicians who are just starting out are focused on establishing themselves and growing their patient base. With time comes a comfortable, consistent patient volume as the practice settles into maturity. When physicians approach retirement age and their interest in practicing wanes, there is often a decline in patient activity. Hospitals are vulnerable to losing these patients as they scatter to other practices that

may or may not be affiliated with the organization. Succession planning for key physicians allows for a more orderly transition as doctors near retirement. The issue is often broached by a loyal doctor who has no exit plan for leaving practice. Hospitals can help keep the patient base intact in at least two ways: by finding another physician to join the practice and eventually buy out the retiring physician, or by recruiting another physician who would like to immediately acquire the practice through an alignment model attractive to both parties.

Insights from this analysis will launch health systems out of the gate and into the field by producing a focused set of tactics to support the overall physician strategy for a service line.

Other channel strategies

Although most marketers would argue, and justifiably so, that physicians are the primary channel through which patients flow, other channels or access points are strategically significant for some service lines. The emergency room, for example, is the entry point for many patients needing cardiac, neuro, or orthopedic care. And many times, patients or their family members make the decision as to when and where to seek emergency care. One hospital discovered that 60% of its acute myocardial infarction patients arrived at the ER by car instead of ambulance. Chest pain evaluation centers attract individuals that may be experiencing some discomfort but can't discern whether it's heartburn or something more serious.

As part of a sports medicine program, one hospital hosts a stress-or-fracture evaluation clinic in its ER on Saturday mornings, following Friday evening school athletic events. Others have successfully built neurology volumes by marketing programs to people with migraine or stroke symptoms.

To boost mammography rates, an east coast health system no longer requires physician orders for women scheduling a screening. Women contact the hospital call center directly to make an appointment. A hospital in the southeast with a successful orthopedic service line marketing program works closely with senior housing, assisted living, and nursing facilities to garner referrals. An analysis of both the origin and entry point of a service line's patient population will reveal the importance of various channels in terms of volume, revenue, and profitability. Assuming that most or all volumes originate from a primary care physician referral to a specialist, and that referral later converts to an admission, may mean missing other important marketing opportunities.

Promotion Strategies

Promotion strategies encompass all demand creation and demand maintenance activities. They are the principal manner in which organizations build brand awareness, convey information about products and services, cultivate consumer interest in offerings, persuade customers to try or buy a service, and communicate points of differentiation. Nearly all methods of promotion can be categorized under the following major headings:

- **Advertising.** This is defined as any paid form of presentation or information by an identified sponsor about a company's goods or services with the intent to cultivate demand for those goods or services. Advertising takes on many forms, including traditional mass media methods, such as television, radio, newsprint, and magazine. It also includes outdoor and display promotions, such as billboards and bus wraps. Direct mail is also a form of advertising that provides great opportunity for targeted promotions. In recent years, more companies are also using online methods of advertising. Many nontraditional methods of paid media are also emerging as advertisers seek more and different ways to break through the hundreds of thousands of messages consumers are bombarded with on an ongoing basis.

- **Sales promotions.** This includes a wide variety of activities to engage consumers with a company, product, or service. Events such as health fairs or risk screenings are a form of sales promotion. It also includes program exhibits, comarketing events, contests, education programs, point-of-service displays, coupons, and other nonroutine sales or promotions efforts. A hospital in the southwest created a comarketing promotion with a national retailer to promote mammography. "Getting a Mammogram Is a Piece of Cake" offered women who showed proof of having had a screening exam a free slice of cake at the upscale retailer's café.

- **Publicity.** This takes on many forms, the most traditional of which is news coverage about a company, product, or service. Most service line marketing efforts leverage publicity tactics to announce program enhancements, the arrival of new physicians, and the addition of new clinical technologies and to promote accreditations, awards, and third-party rankings such as *U.S. News & World Report*'s Top 100 Hospitals list. Some service line marketing programs have developed an active speaker's bureau highlighting their physicians, clinical experts, and even patients willing to talk about their healthcare experiences.

- **e-Marketing.** Also known as digital marketing, this is defined as the use of the Internet and related digital information and communication technologies to achieve marketing objectives. Almost all hospitals feature information about key service line offerings on health system–sponsored websites; some produce microsites for major clinical programs. Today, however, e-marketing reaches far beyond the hospital website. Service line marketers must also consider their broader Web presence. Social media marketing has emerged as a targeted means by which to engage consumers of like interests and needs. How marketers find, reach, listen to, communicate with, and build service line brands with specific online communities is a new marketing art form, and one that is producing great results when meaningfully employed.
- **Sales and physician referral development.** Many service lines approach physician referral development through a formal physician relations program staffed by physician representatives or liaisons. Physician representatives are trained in sales and referral development, and are charged with developing relationships with physicians that result in increased business for the clinical service line. Sometimes these programs

are organized and managed by health system marketing departments, sometimes the physician representative is employed by the service line, and occasionally they have some other reporting relationship.

Without a specific plan for how service line volumes will be built through physician referrals, the overall strategy for the service line is likely to falter. This requires a clear understanding of which physicians refer business today and how referral patterns have changed or are likely to change. Typical referral development tactics address:

- ***High-volume specialists*** who practice exclusively at your hospital—maintaining good working relationships and quickly resolving problems are critical to retaining high-volume specialists. The physician representative can identify and help address dissatisfaction issues, solicit ideas for extending service line offerings or programs with potential to bring in additional volume, or facilitate the introduction of specialists to primary care doctors.
- Specialists who practice at your hospital but also take some business to competing service providers—for "***splitters***," the physician liaison should try to discover what it would take to admit more of these physicians' patients to the service line, and work with the service line leaders to meet those needs and build the trust and confidence to gain these physicians' business.
- ***Primary care physicians*** and other subspecialists who refer patients to service line specialists or diagnostic or treatment services—many clinical programs and specialists still rely on patient referrals from primary care physicians. Today, many primary care physicians no

longer practice in the hospital and don't know or have loyal relationships with specialists. In this case, a key role for the physician representative is to educate primary care physicians about the services, clinical expertise, and capabilities of the physician specialists who provide care.

Case study: The art and science of database segmentation marketing

Borgess Health offers a complete continuum of healthcare services to approximately 1.1 million people living in 11 counties in southwest Michigan. It is comprised of more than 130 care sites in 15 cities, including nine owned or affiliated hospitals, a cancer center, a nursing home, ambulatory care facilities, physician practices, managed care and home healthcare services, as well as an air ambulance service. Borgess is known and acclaimed for its centers of excellence in cardiology, neurosciences, orthopedics, and vascular care.

For years, Borgess had been engaging in more traditional marketing tactics to promote its programs and services, including print advertising, radio, television, direct mail, and community education classes. People responding to its various campaigns were then entered into the Borgess database for tracking purposes. Marketing leadership also viewed every touchpoint, such as health fitness center memberships and special events like fun runs and fundraisers as an opportunity to build the Borgess database.

The system has a long history as an early adopter of electronic applications offered by the Internet. For example, Borgess has been offering online requests for appointments and physician referrals for nearly 10 years, as well as electronic prescription renewals through its website. So it was a logical evolution when, in 2006, Borgess began devoting more attention to leveraging the use of its database for more effective and efficient marketing. The timing was right. With the rise in popularity of using the Internet to connect with people "real-time" through social networking sites, blogs, and podcasts, the opportunities for reaching out electronically were multiplying rapidly. The Borgess website offered a robust means of connecting with potential patients on an interactive basis.

Borgess currently has more than one million names in the marketing database, thanks to its efforts in collecting consumer information at every touchpoint. Using a vendor partner who overlays sophisticated psychographic segmentation criteria to the database—there are 56 different psychographic profiles in all—marketing leadership can create highly targeted lists of names and e-mail addresses of people most likely to use a particular service.

For instance, when Borgess rolled out its Bone and Joint Institute in 2010, it could easily create a database of older athletes in a certain neighborhood and income level, who read particular sports-oriented magazines, participate in high impact sports, and are at risk of needing a joint replacement. So the system created service line-specific e-mail contact programs that target a certain demographic.

Push e-newsletters are sent on a regular basis and have become the mainstay of Borgess marketing efforts, along with direct mail to highly segmented lists. A partnership with a local TV affiliate yields regular two-minute news segments on pertinent health topics, and those videos are then added to the Borgess website.

In addition, Borgess has invested heavily in its electronic presence via a Facebook page, Twitter account, and YouTube channel, which serves as another repository of the news segment videos. Hundreds of people have subscribed to Borgess RSS feeds to keep up-to-date on the latest system events and programs. The open rate of Borgess e-newsletters is as high as 30%—well above traditional direct mail response rates.

According to marketing leadership, having the database of contacts allows for easier calculations of return on investment for marketing expenditures. For instance, the system sponsors a Borgess Run Camp for potential participants in its annual "Run for the Health of It" event every year. In 2009, participants' fees paid for the expenses to put on the Run Camp. Downstream revenue from participants over the past four years totals more than $275,000.

Borgess has successfully adopted database segmentation strategies to market its services and meet the needs of consumers in the marketplace. The system is well at the forefront of an evolving marketing strategy that continually engages potential patients who have already expressed interest in the Borgess brand.

Payers, Pricing, and Performance

Pricing strategies are rarely addressed in service line marketing plans because of the prevalence of third-party reimbursement for the vast majority of service line patients. Cost-based pricing systems prevalent in hospitals are largely the domain of the finance department, which establishes the charge master and negotiates rates with third-party payers. Insured consumers rarely see the list price or negotiated rates, and payers set their copayments and deductibles. The principal goal of hospital pricing and contract negotiation with insurers is profitable reimbursement: recovery of the cost of labor, supplies, and other expenses to provide patient care with a positive contribution margin. Service line managers and marketers should work closely with finance to establish rates, support negotiations to achieve target reimbursement levels, and manage aggressively to optimize margins.

Increasingly, government and private insurers will initiate pay-for-performance and value-based reimbursement models. For health systems and hospitals, this trend signals a fundamental shift in the basis for competition in the industry—and will require a deeper comprehension of pricing, contracting, and cost management from service line leaders, marketing professionals, and finance experts alike. Service line marketing strategies must consider payer mix (the percentage of revenues provided by different payer sources) and prescribe tactical direction for optimally achieving growth in those payer segments that will improve service line financial performance.

In recent years, hospitals have experienced an increasing number of consumers inquiring about prices for certain procedures or tests. The number of inquiries increased in accordance with greater numbers of people enrolling in health savings accounts and high-deductible health plans. Many health systems are also diversifying into the retail services arena to capture consumer discretionary spending for items ranging from fitness to cosmetic surgery to alternative medicine. Hospitals with weight-loss or bariatric surgery programs may look at bundled pricing for consumers who pay cash for the service. Some also provide low-interest financing through partnerships with banks or other financial institutions. The greatest challenge for most healthcare organizations when it comes to consumer pricing models is understanding price as a vehicle to establish value, rather than just recover cost. The complexity of living in multiple worlds—regulated reimbursement, negotiated contracts, and competitive market pricing—will demand greater-than-ever alignment of brand, product, channel, and customer marketing processes with pricing decisions.

Summary

Service line marketing planning is essential to identifying market opportunities, choosing those with the best growth potential, and aligning and gaining commitment across the organization for resources to achieve success. The service line marketing plan—at a strategic level—provides the foundation for determining specific initiatives, tactics, and investments to achieve results. It should define and address the competitive challenges and opportunities for the service line, identify and size those markets and high impact customer segments that will drive growth and improve profitability, and articulate the specific value proposition for each key segment. The strategic marketing plan should also address the distinct mix of strategies for differentiation, physician engagement, access, customer experience, pricing, contracting, promotions, and other marketing initiatives to improve competitive performance.

References

Baker, Stuart; Eaton, Michael; Miller, Jeff. "Five "Rs" Provide a Framework for Physician Alignment." Navvis & Company, April 2010.

Bryant, Carla; Corrigan, Karen; Eaton, Michael. "The Business of Brands: Growth. Innovation. Leverage." Navvis & Company, March 2010.

Corrigan, Karen. "The Price Is Right." *Marketing Health Services*. American Medical Association, Fall 2006.

Scott, David M. *The New Rules of Marketing and PR*. Wiley, 2010.

Trout, Jack; Ries, Al. *Positioning: The Battle for Your Mind*. McGraw-Hill, 2000.

CHAPTER 4

Developing the Service Line Marketing Plan

A comprehensive, written, and detailed marketing plan provides an overall road map for implementing, managing, and adapting the service line marketing strategy. Without one, health systems tend to chase ad hoc activities based on a competitor's latest move or the well-meaning but unfocused whim of a physician or operations leader. This results in inconsistent actions, otherwise known as the "campaign of the month" syndrome, and wastes marketing dollars. Worse, it can leave a health system susceptible to brand, volume, and market share erosion over time. Taking a planned approach to the marketplace based on market intelligence, good strategic thinking, purposeful execution, and organizational commitment to sustained initiatives will keep marketers, service line leaders, physicians, and administrators focused on the actions and investments to grow the business.

Engaging Operational, Clinical, and Physician Leaders

Although marketing accountability typically lies with the health system's chief marketing executive, effective service line marketing requires the engagement and support of C-suite administrators, operations and service line managers, physician leaders, and other key stakeholders. Marketing, together with operations, physicians, nursing, purchasing, IT, finance, and human resources comprise a cross-functional, customer-focused, and growth-oriented service line ecosystem where each player holds an important and distinctive role in the overall success of service line marketing initiatives.

Collaboration among this group is critical to the service line marketing planning process. By working together to identify market opportunities and threats, the team develops a common knowledge base, understanding, and belief about how marketing forces are likely to unfold. When establishing and agreeing upon growth targets and goals, a sense of shared accountability for those goals takes root. During the strategy formulation stage, the interdependency of marketing and operations is played out as the team debates and comes to agreement on the critical strategic elements to drive results.

Even more important, when marketing initiatives are launched, the hospital must be ready to respond to inquiries, referrals, and changes in volume resulting from marketing activities. It may seem elementary, but something as simple as having a call center to take, qualify, and convert leads into appointments is too often missing in implementation. Marketing expenditures that pique consumer interest are wasted resources if prospective customers are lost because there's no structure and process to convert them into actual customers.

Other key areas where marketing strategy and operational implementation must be aligned include:

- Availability and timeliness of appointments
- Location, hours of operation, and convenience of access points
- Capacity, patient flow, and through-put (e.g., ERs, ORs, ambulatory care)
- Clinical quality, safety, and outcomes
- Staffing, training, and accountability for customer service
- Facilities, technology, and equipment
- Information systems, electronic health records, Web-enabled communications, and transactions
- Availability, efficacy, and costs of medical devices and supplies

Key structural and process elements are required to create shared ownership and accountability for marketing activities that drive service line growth and profitability. The most successful execution of a service line marketing plan acknowledges a fundamental change in how hospitals have traditionally determined roles, responsibilities, and commitment to marketing. Marketing initiatives—*and investments*—that are endorsed by the CEO and other executive suite leaders have the greatest potential for success. (See Figure 4.1 for an example of an interdisciplinary service line marketing committee). Other necessary elements include the following:

- A team orientation, co-led by marketing and service line operations, that engages other administrative and clinical leaders

- An organizational commitment to initiatives and investments directed toward targeted service line growth and profitability metrics
- Communication to all stakeholders within the organization, including frontline staff responsible for delivering care and services to customers
- Product, program, and operational readiness, including systems and processes for customer contact, conversion, and relationship management
- Authority and accountability for results flowing between and among marketing and administrative and clinical team members

FIGURE 4.1

EXAMPLE OF INTERDISCIPLINARY SERVICE LINE MARKETING COMMITTEE PARTICIPATION

Create shared accountability for results across marketing, clinical, and business operations.

Marketing Team	Clinical Team	Business Team
Marketing Management	Service Line Executive	Business Development
Marketing Communications	Physician Leaders/VPMA	Operations Leaders
Marketing Research	Nursing Managers	Finance Executives
Physician Relations & Sales	Patient Care Coordinators	Supply Chain Managers
Public Relations	Ambulatory Care Managers	Information Systems
Events Marketing	Ancillary Services Directors	Registration Systems

Together, Accountable for Results

Meet regularly; establish shared purpose and accountabilities.
Assess, discuss, and understand competitive issues and opportunities.
Establish, agree upon, and recommend growth goals and objectives.
Contribute to development of strategies, tactics, and action plans.
Collaborate on execution; monitor progress; make course corrections.

Communication to stakeholders

Successful implementation of a service line marketing strategy begins with educating those who have a stake in its execution. It is predicated on communication of the timing and content of the strategy to internal clinicians, administrators, physicians, and staff who may be affected by any messages introduced to the market. It also requires sharing not only the strategy and action plan that will be pursued, but also the crucial strategic results and metrics that have to be met for the initiative to be successful. By developing a stakeholder communications plan, you can ensure that associates are best prepared to do their part in executing the plan for results and support the marketing initiatives in their respective roles.

Key topics to address with stakeholder audiences include:

- An overview of the trends, market dynamics, and competitive issues affecting the service line
- A description of the health system's plans for continued growth and development of the service line (e.g., adding new services, acquiring a new technology, recruiting new physicians)
- Service line goals—volume growth, revenue and margin targets, and market position
- Overview of the marketing strategy, goals, and objectives—segments, programs, and methods
- Review of marketing promotions and sales activities, and a schedule for when those will occur

- How consumer responses will be handled in terms of information, appointments, referrals, and walk-in business
- Specifically, how stakeholders can support the marketing plan and activities

Ideally, members of the cross-functional service line marketing team will participate in stakeholder communications sessions.

Setting Marketing Goals and Objectives

The service line marketing plan should specifically state the organization's overall strategic goals for the clinical program, its financial objectives and desired outcomes, and return on marketing investments. Goals and objectives should be carefully quantified, especially in terms of achievable outcomes such as volume, revenue, market share, and customer satisfaction or loyalty.

Objectives should be informed by the market opportunity assessment, an analysis of the organization's capacity and ability to add additional volume, and the strategic and financial goals of the health system's strategic plan. Objectives should stretch the organization, but also be reasonable and attainable. Service line marketing objectives usually include both short- and long-term goals, and fall into the following key sets.

Strategic goals

Strategic objectives and performance metrics often have a longer horizon point (e.g., three years) and are aimed at the service line's overall measure of competitiveness. Examples of strategic goals/metrics include:

- Market position (e.g., "to be the leading provider of cardiovascular care in the greater metropolitan market"), which can be measured by market share growth
- Brand position (e.g., "to be the preferred brand of sports medicine by female athletes"), measured by consumer preference and loyalty
- Service line reputation (e.g., "to be recognized as a top 100 hospital for neurology"), measured by third-party recognitions

Financial goals

Financial objectives address service line revenue and profitability targets, as well as expectations for return on investments. The service line may have both short- and long-term financial goals aimed at both revenue growth and cost efficiency. Examples of service line financial goals/metrics include:

- Service line net revenues (e.g., "produce net revenues of $*x* million over *x* [period of time]")
- Service line margin (e.g., "achieve a *x*% margin on operating revenues")
- Payer mix (e.g., "grow commercial volumes by *x*%")
- Cost reduction (e.g., "reduce supply cost of orthopedic implants by *x*%")

Marketing goals

Marketing goals are quantitative translations of the service line's strategic and financial objectives, expressed in marketing terms. Marketing goals can have both short-term (e.g., one year) and longer-term (e.g., three years) targets. Too often, unfortunately, marketing goals are stated in activity terms versus outcomes. Outcomes and activity metrics are both important, but they serve different purposes. Examples of activity metrics include measures such as advertising insertions, reach, and frequency; call center volumes and Web inquiries; event registrations and attendance; and so on. These metrics tell us something about the effectiveness of various marketing tactics and, with more sophisticated modeling analytics, can determine the volume and types of responses required to achieve the following outcomes objectives:

- Overall service line volume growth
- Growth in specific service line diagnosis-related groups
- Rate of growth vis-à-vis the market
- Changes in market share
- Increases in volume or share by target market segment
- Changes in payer mix
- Increases in consumer awareness and preference

Establishing and gaining agreement on strategic, financial, and marketing goals—and the performance metrics for those goals—is a critical up-front objective in service line marketing planning. Marketing strategy and investments must be tailored to achieve the goals, and measurement systems established to inform all involved as to the business success of major marketing activities and investments.

Focus Marketing Measurement on Strategic and Financial Outcomes

If marketing is to be valued as a core service line investment, then the marketing officer must instill a rigorous, results-oriented discipline to set quantifiable goals and demonstrate return on investment. Too often, marketing goals are either missing in action or stated in terms too "soft" to get the CFO's endorsement. Performance measurements are often activity- or process-oriented, which, while important for managing an efficient marketing operation, don't always link expenditures to business outcomes.

The bottom line is this: in the C-suite, only two sets of metrics count—results related to financial performance and results related to strategic performance. Revenue. Volume growth. Market share. Profitability. Brand loyalty. Differentiation. Competitive sustainability.

We all know the challenges faced by service line marketers when it comes to ROI—information systems that aren't oriented to customer transactions or purchasing patterns, extensive variations in pricing and reimbursement, complex channel relationships, long buying cycles, etc. However, marketing accountability for performance is often derailed at three junctions:

1. **Production of marketing plans that are really tactical "to do" lists confined to marketing department activities.** Many a marketing effort falters because actions are created and dollars expended without the strategic underpinning that aligns the organization's growth goals with market opportunities. This happens when marketing is disconnected from growth discussions, then called in after the fact to put a communications spin on the decision-making. A strategic marketing plan is a derivative of the company's strategic plan, addressing how the health system intends to grow, what markets it will serve and with what products and services, how it will create differentiation and sources of competitive advantage, how brands will be positioned, how the portfolio will be configured to optimize profitability, how marketing investments will be prioritized, and what the expectations are for returns.

2. **Marketing investments that overemphasize marketing promotions as the primary customer acquisition strategy.** At a recent gathering of healthcare marketing executives, the chief marketing officer for a well-known, national electronics retailer shared the business analytics that framed his company's marketing strategy and modeled how he could project (with great accuracy) changes in sales and profitability by manipulating various aspects of the brand strategy and marketing mix. What he demonstrated was how a strategic balance of marketing investments focused on segmentation and targeting, product development, market expansion, channel relationships, pricing, customer experience, and, yes, promotion were required to drive business outcomes. This means an investment in

research methodologies that go beyond the awareness-preference studies so prevalent in our industry, and integrated business, operational, clinical, brand, and marketing strategies that encompass more than promotions.

3. **Lack of ownership at the executive team level for marketing performance.** The nexus of the problem may well reside here if marketing is simply viewed as a functional department and not as a core business discipline and competitive competency of the organization. A marketing orientation is derived from an organizational culture centered on customer needs as well as the sum of organizational activities designed to create profitable exchange relationships by fulfilling those needs. Marketing department activities have limited utility when access, capacity, pricing, products, customer service, clinical quality, physician relationships, and other operational aspects of the business are out of whack. It's critical for the CMO, with the CEO, to spread co-ownership of the marketing goals, strategy, and investments—and coaccountability for delivery and performance outcomes—across the entire executive team.

The endgame is customer engagement that results in service line growth, profitability and sustainability. But without full engagement of the organization's leaders in establishing marketing performance targets, strategies, and investments—and without agreement as to the strategic and financial metrics that spell success—the service line marketer is left to defend marketing department activities and expenditures that appear discretionary, rather than essential, to winning in the marketplace.

Content of a Service Line Marketing Plan

Different healthcare organizations use different outlines or frameworks for marketing plans. The outline that follows describes, in general terms, the key content of the planning document. The marketing plan is simply a written description of the objectives, strategies, and tactics for the service line. The plan itself it not a strategy, but rather a road map for how the strategy is to be implemented, monitored, and controlled.

Most hospitals and health systems develop individual and more extensive service line marketing plans for their top-tier programs, aligned to the business objectives for growth of those key programs. Those programs of a lesser priority in terms of growth and investment may be supported by less intense, maintenance-level marketing activities.

The following are basic constructs of a service line marketing plan.

Executive summary

The executive summary provides an abbreviated overview of the proposed plan, highlighting the market opportunities and challenges, service line goals and marketing objectives, summary of major initiatives, investments, and expected return on marketing investment. This high-level summary addresses:

- Service line business objectives
- Growth opportunities and competitive challenges
- Major marketing strategies and programs

- Marketing, operating, and investment requirements
- Projected results

Marketing situation

This section provides relevant information about the past history, evolution, and current state of the service line in regards to its market position, reputation, breadth and depth of service offerings, geographic presence, new and planned expansions, new program development, physician alignment, competitive assessment, and macro-environmental trends that could influence or dramatically shift demand for services. It covers:

- A description of the service line and its role and contribution to health system performance
- Services offered and markets served
- Historical perspective, trended performance, and current position (e.g., rate of growth, share, volume, revenue, contribution margins)
- New developments or plans for expansion of facilities, services, or capabilities
- Physician supply, capacity, geographic distribution, alignment, and loyalty
- Service line competitors, size of operations, strengths, and vulnerabilities
- Macro-environmental and health industry trends (e.g., new technologies, changes in reimbursement, population aging)

Opportunity assessment

The opportunity assessment specifically addresses market opportunities and threats aimed at growth, profitability, customer responsiveness, physician loyalty, technology advancements, reimbursement, and other factors that have the potential to affect business performance for the service line. This section should also describe the hospital and service line strengths and weaknesses relevant to acting on opportunities or defending against threats, such as:

- Population growth and distribution
- Risk factors, incidence rates, and utilization patterns
- Demand analysis and projections
- Market attractiveness in terms of size, growth, reimbursement, and advancements in technology
- Identification of unmet needs offering growth opportunities
- Regulatory, reimbursement, and policy changes
- Recent or potential new market entrants (e.g., an out-of-market health system acquires a local competitor or a niche provider builds a service line–focused ambulatory center)

Marketing objectives

Strategic, financial, and marketing goals are summarized in this section. Objectives should be challenging enough to create a bias for action, yet realistic based upon industry, market, and organization dynamics. Marketing objectives should include:

- Strategic goals (e.g., position, share, brand, competitive sustainability)
- Financial goals (e.g., revenue, margin, ROI)
- Marketing goals (e.g., volume growth, rate of growth by segment, consumer preference)

Marketing strategies

This section provides the overall description of the various strategies that will be employed to achieve service line marketing objectives. This is the overall game plan for growing the business. It should describe the decisions made about target markets, service line positioning and branding, clinical offerings, channel relationships, physician alignment and referral development, geographic presence and reach, contracting and pricing, and promotions and sales. Include:

- Target market segments (e.g., size, growth, needs, expectations)
- Service line positioning overall and by segment (e.g., capabilities, distinctiveness, benefits)
- Marketing mix by target segment (e.g., product, distribution, pricing, promotion)
- Physicians, access points, and other referral channels (e.g., primary care physicians, ERs, urgent care clinics, skilled nursing facilities, health plans, employers)
- Sales and promotional activities (e.g., advertising, marketing events, social media marketing, referral development)

Action plans

Detailed plans should be developed to guide implementation of the marketing strategy—what tactics will be employed? By whom? When? What resources (financial and otherwise) will be required? Consider:

- Marketing tactics, activities, and tasks
- A timeline for implementation
- The parties responsible for development, implementation, and management of tasks, including external resources, such as market research firms, advertising agencies, Web developers, etc.
- Marketing budget and allocations
- Marketing operations and management systems, such as call centers and customer relationship management processes

Sales and revenue projections

Here you should provide a summary of the expected changes in volume, revenue, payer mix, and other outcomes metrics resulting from the marketing strategy, and assess the projected return on the investment required to launch and sustain the plan:

- Projected changes
  - Volumes
  - Revenues
  - Reimbursement levels
  - Operating costs from changes in volume
- Summary of marketing and related business development expenditures
- Projected return on marketing investment

Monitoring and controls

This final element provides details as to how results will be monitored, measured, and reported, as well as how often the plan will be reviewed and adjusted. This is also a good place to detail potential risks (e.g., a major physician group leaving for a competitor organization) and the process for continuous monitoring of the ever-changing market and competitive dynamics. Be sure to cover:

- Metrics, measurement methods, and intervals
- Reporting mechanisms, such as a service line marketing dashboard
- Frequency of plan review and renewal
- Risks and contingencies

Service Line Marketing Performance Management

Once the goals are set, the plan is done, the budget is approved, and a green light is given for implementation, marketing and service line leaders must continue to work in concert to achieve service line growth goals. Marketing executives will manage a number of specific initiatives focused on brand management, new product development, physician referral development and sales, advertising campaigns, direct marketing, and other activities focused on cultivating demand, increasing inquiries, and converting that to new business.

Some hospitals have designated marketing managers for key service lines given the millions of dollars of revenue and profitability that major clinical programs can contribute to healthcare organizations. The service line marketing manager directs all aspects of marketing planning, execution, and management in collaboration with service line business and clinical operations. A sample job description for a service line marketing manager can be found in Figure 4.2.

FIGURE 4.2

SERVICE LINE MARKETING MANAGER SAMPLE JOB DESCRIPTION

Position Description
The service line marketing manager is responsible for developing, implementing, and monitoring marketing strategies, plans, and programs to achieve growth and revenue goals. The manager monitors and communicates trends and market conditions that influence demand for service line offerings. He or she is also responsible for developing and recommending marketing strategies, programs, and investments to increase volume, revenue, and competitive performance. In addition, the manager should be able to build a coalition of support and shared accountability for achievement of growth goals.

Accountabilities:

- Research and Assessment. Monitors service line trends and assesses changes in the competitive environment. Identifies growth opportunities and competitive challenges. Develops, commissions, and uses market research to support marketing decision-making and service line planning.
- Marketing Planning. Responsible for creating and implementing marketing plans for assigned service line. Includes and engages physician, clinical, and operational participation in marketing planning. Gains organizational commitment and secures resources to support the plan.
- Marketing Implementation. Leads the development, launch, and management of marketing initiatives, promotions, sales, referral development, and other marketing programs to achieve service line volume and revenue goals. Mobilizes system-wide teams and physicians to accomplish objectives. Works with outside vendors and business partners (e.g. call centers, advertising agencies).
- Brand Management. Supports development and growth of the service line brand in the context of the health system's brand strategy and structure. Builds service line brand distinctiveness, awareness, preference, and loyalty.
- Marketing Management. Monitors, measures, and reports results and return on marketing investments. Recommends changes in strategy and course corrections.

Service line managers, along with other administrative, clinical, and physician leaders, will build and develop service line offerings, clinical capabilities, new technologies and programs; support the recruitment of and build relationships with physicians; lead quality, safety, and patient-satisfaction improvement initiatives; monitor and work with staff to create efficient, effective, customer-centered operations; and deliver the patient experience critical to building the service line's reputation and repeat business.

The overall effectiveness of the service line marketing plan is highly dependent upon this level of focused effort at creating and delivering a quality, differentiated product. See Figure 4.3 for creating shared accountability for service line marketing management.

Summary

Committing the service line marketing strategy to writing is a critical aspect of effective marketing management. The written plan is a powerful tool for building internal understanding of the analysis and rationale for decisions; gaining commitment to a focused course of action and investment requirements; detailing the actions, timelines, and accountabilities for implementation; and articulating how key performance indicators will be tracked, measured, and reported. When marketing planning includes the participation and engagement of operational, clinical, financial, and marketing professionals, there is greater shared accountability for its execution and results.

FIGURE 4.3

CREATING SHARED ACCOUNTABILITY FOR SERVICE LINE MARKETING MANAGEMENT

	Accountability to Service Line Marketing	Expectations from Service Line Marketer
Chief Executive Officer	Executive support to build a service line marketing management competency and culture aligned to the health system's vision, strategy, and growth goals.	Marketing leadership to define, design, and execute strategies and initiatives that drive service line growth and competitive performance.
Service Line Administrator	Leadership to support and champion development and implementation of the service line marketing strategy; delivery of consistent, accessible, high quality clinical and patient care services; clinical programming and new service development; cultivation of physician relationships to support access and referrals.	Data, insights, strategies, programs, resources, marketing expertise, and collaborative planning processes to guide service line decisions regarding growth priorities, physician referral and contracting relationships, and patient experience.
Chief Physician Executive	Clinical leadership for development and delivery of high quality medical care, continuous quality improvement, patient experience, clinical programming, and physician alignment and engagement.	Information, collaboration, and support for continuous development and improvement of service line offerings, patient experience design, physician engagement, and referral development.
Chief Financial Officer	Data and support to better understand opportunities, prioritize marketing resources, and track return on marketing investment; and funding to build the service line marketing infrastructure and support the development and execution of marketing strategies.	Market analysis and planning to identify and recommend high impact growth initiatives and prioritize service line marketing resource investments against system objectives; and accountability for effective and efficient use of resources and return on marketing investment.

FIGURE 4.3 (CONT.)

CREATING SHARED ACCOUNTABILITY FOR SERVICE LINE MARKETING MANAGEMENT

	Accountability to Service Line Marketing	Expectations from Service Line Marketer
Chief Information Officer	Information systems that capture and provide data to inform marketing decision-making, facilitate communications with patients and referral sources, and support eMarketing via Web and social marketing strategies.	Collaboration to define and develop the needed functionalities, data sources, strategies, and practices to better leverage technology for service line marketing management.
Chief Marketing Officer	Leadership to establish overall health system and service line growth and marketing priorities; advocate for and obtain strategy-critical resources; define the knowledge, capabilities and skill requirements of a high performing service line marketing operation; develop support for creation of a marketing culture.	Development, implementation, and monitoring of comprehensive service line marketing plans and initiatives aligned to growth objectives; achievement of volume, revenue, and strategic marketing goals; efficient use of marketing resources; collaborative cross-functional service line marketing management.

References

Farris, Paul W.; Bender, Neil; Pfiefer, Philip; Reibstein, David. *Marketing Metrics: 50+ Metrics Every Executive Should Master.* Wharton School Publishing, 2006.

Kotler, Philip. *Strategic Marketing for Health Care Organizations: Building a Customer-Driven Health System.* Jossey-Bass, 2008.

Kotler, Philip; Keller, Kevin. *Marketing Management,* 13th Edition. Prentice-Hall, Inc., 2008.

Thomas, Richard K. *Health Services Marketing.* Springer, 2007.

CHAPTER 5

Service Line Marketing Case Studies

Service line marketing strategies can vary significantly from organization to organization. Some pursue mass marketing to build brand presence and appeal to a broad segment of the population, while others employ more targeted techniques to reach and attract niche markets. Some organizations put greater emphasis on physician alignment and others focus on cultivating consumer engagement. What counts at the end of the day is whether the strategy or mix of strategies achieved the marketing objectives.

The following pages provide brief snapshots of different marketing approaches pursued by health systems for clinical service lines common across many organizations—cardiovascular, oncology, orthopedics, neurosciences, women's health, and general surgery.

Cardiovascular Service Line Marketing

The cardiovascular service line is one of the most important clinical programs for many health systems because cardiovascular disease (CVD) ranks highest among all disease categories for hospital discharges. One out of every six hospital stays results from CVD, and it accounts for one-fourth of the total costs of hospital care in the United States. One in three American adults has one or more types of CVD, such as coronary heart disease, stroke, and high blood pressure, according to the American Heart Association's "Heart Disease and Stroke Statistics—2010 Update." As the aging baby boomer population gets older, it is expected to increase demand for cardiovascular care, while diabetes as a comorbidity will add complexity to cardiovascular treatment. Within all major categories of CVD, around a fifth of patients also have diabetes, and the proportion is growing.

The umbrella of cardiac services includes medical cardiology, cardiac surgery, interventional cardiology, and electrophysiology. CVD procedures will continue to be key volume and margin performers since they drive high utilization of imaging and procedural services. However, advances in treatment are driving a decline in inpatient surgeries and a corresponding increase in outpatient procedures. For example, coronary artery bypass surgery has declined significantly due to clinical advances moving the procedure from the surgery suite to the cath lab. In addition, cardiovascular programs are increasingly pressured to perform cases in the outpatient setting as the federal government seeks to lower the cost of care delivery and scrutinizes appropriateness of inpatient admissions.

Overall, cardiac catheter procedures and cardiac medicine volumes are projected to decline 16% and 7%, respectively, through 2018; while electrophysiology procedures and cardiac surgery are expected to increase by 23% and 5%, respectively, during the same time period.

Due to the high prevalence of CVD and the accompanying high volume of services, clinical studies continue to be published showing treatment advances or disappointments in cardiac health outcomes. These evidence-based results lead to changes in how cardiac care is delivered. Thus, in addition to competitive pressures, softening volumes, and technology challenges, the cardiac service line has come under scrutiny as a means to measure hospital performance.

Health systems with strong cardiovascular programs often seek to leverage overall brand equity through the reputation of their cardiovascular service line. Niche marketing strategies are also effective. In recent years, many hospitals have developed programs that focus on women's heart health or appeal to people with diabetes who are at high risk for heart disease. Risk screenings remain popular outreach tactics because they are effective at identifying people in need of evaluation or intervention, and the results are easy to track and report. Support groups, which have always been popular for those with heart disease, are now moving online, and hospitals are creating innovative approaches to engage patients through social media networks.

Case study: Building the service line brand—WellStar Cardiac Network

WellStar Health System in Marietta, GA, was established in 1993 when five community-based hospitals joined together to create one of the area's first health systems. In addition to its hospitals, the nonprofit organization is composed of urgent care centers, imaging centers, and allied physicians' offices covering four counties in rural and suburban Georgia. Despite its longevity as a health system, WellStar had never attempted to market a service line as a system, opting instead to market individual services at each of its hospitals. For instance, its flagship hospital had been promoting its heart surgery partnership with Emory University, and three WellStar hospitals were touting their accredited chest pain centers. That changed in 2009, when WellStar acquired a large cardiovascular practice aimed at building the system's overall cardiac volume throughout its catchment areas.

WellStar's marketing leadership team conducted consumer research to determine a baseline level of awareness and how to best position the system's cardiac programs in the marketplace. Consumers seemed less able to identify with the term *institute*, but the concept of a network resonated well and was more easily understood. With a full continuum of services—from prevention, imaging, interventional services, surgical care, and rehabilitation—WellStar had all of the elements in place to promote just such a network.

In mid-2009, WellStar introduced its first systemwide service line campaign, "We Believe in Heart," to create awareness of its cardiac network. The campaign highlighted actual patients who had suffered a cardiac event and survived, thanks to WellStar clinicians. Marketing leadership employed a variety of tactics during the campaign, including TV, radio, and print advertising and billboards. The team is also using sophisticated segmentation strategies to target 5,000 households per month via direct mailings to promote its cardiac screening. The database uses predictive modeling and psychographics to identify those individuals who may be more at risk for a cardiac event.

In addition to the awareness campaign, WellStar introduced a low-dose cardiac screening program that could identify a respondent's risk for a future cardiac event. Conducted at WellStar's imaging centers, the screening served as a non-threatening point of entry for patients to experience WellStar's cardiac services. And it saved lives in the process: 75% of the 960 people screened as of May 2010 had a positive finding of some health issue. Those patients were then referred to a WellStar physician for follow-up.

Case study: Focusing on the basics—Christiana Care's Center for Heart & Vascular Health

Serving the people of Delaware and neighboring states of Maryland, Pennsylvania, and New Jersey, Christiana Care Health System is composed of two hospitals, a home health care organization, and outpatient services. In spring 2007, Christiana Care opened its Center for Heart & Vascular Health in a new, five-story hospital wing and recruited a nationally recognized heart surgeon and leader in cardiovascular medicine to serve as its medical director. The hospital's new director of marketing saw an unprecedented opportunity to establish Christiana Care as a destination for heart care.

The overarching goal of the marketing plan was to increase consumer awareness of Christiana Care's cardiovascular program by engaging consumers to assess their own heart risks, while building the system's marketing database. The marketing team knew they were starting from scratch and had an excellent opportunity to build name awareness for this key service line. A new call center was established that would serve as the collection point for consumer inquiries and the repository of demographic information on respondents to marketing activities. The marketing team then developed several key initiatives that would drive consumer inquiries to the call center.

To help consumers assess their own cardiovascular risk, the marketing team and the center's clinical leadership engaged a vendor to provide online heart screenings. Respondents could complete a 10-question heart risk assessment that would generate a personalized analysis and printout with recommendations for lowering the risk of a cardiovascular event. Those who completed the assessment could then request a follow-up appointment with a nurse practitioner specializing in cardiac care and receive a personal assessment at the hospital, free of charge. During the appointment, people could obtain information on Christiana Care's heart program, be referred to programs that might mitigate risk factors, or be referred to a cardiologist for follow-up intervention, when necessary.

In addition, the marketing team developed a free heart health kit that included a pedometer, cookbook, information on heart attack, a magnet, and more. The goal was to help people understand how to reduce their risk of heart disease while keeping Christian Care's heart center top of mind.

Before engaging in any advertising to promote the online assessment and heart health kit, all advertising materials were pretested with consumer focus groups, which resulted in the selection of a creative approach emphasizing the consumer perspective ("It's all about *me*") versus the institutional perspective ("Look at our facilities and staff"). The feedback collected from focus groups revealed that their constituents responded to advertising messages that addressed consumer needs—not traditional institutional messaging. Elements of the heart health kit were also tested with focus groups to maximize its appeal to consumers. Christiana Care then chose a variety of tactics to get the word out, including print and radio advertising, direct mail, and public relations. The call center carefully tracked the metrics to determine which marketing tools provided the best returns for their advertising investment. The promotion also helped to create a database of consumers who have an interest in heart health topics.

The due diligence of the market research efforts paid off. Christiana Care had created 2,000 heart health kits for distribution, but requests for the kit topped 10,000 in only two months. While Christiana Care projected that 2,000 people would complete the online assessment, 5,000 have done so as of May 2010, and of these, 750 have scheduled a follow-up screening. Of the patients who have completed a screening, 132 were identified as needing a medical intervention of some kind.

The advertising also enabled Christiana Care to build a database of 10,000 people who had expressed an interest in heart programs via one of the health system's campaigns. Careful tracking of responses and keeping the database "pristine" has also paid off: Christiana Care's direct mail response rate is 12%. By collecting e-mail addresses as part of the campaign, the marketing team has been able to focus on low-cost, blast e-mail campaigns and drop media such as radio, which is mentioned less frequently by those who call the call center as a way of hearing about the program. The results of the e-mail campaigns have also exceeded expectations. A blast e-mail promoting the assessment and follow-up to 8,000 addresses yielded 171 requests for an appointment within the first 36 hours. So the nursing staff conducting the follow-up appointments are not overwhelmed, the marketing department now limits e-mail blasts to 1,000 at a time.

According to marketing leadership, getting back to basics by conducting market research ahead of time—and analyzing incoming data to refine tactics on an ongoing basis—have been the key to meeting the goals set for the Center for Heart & Vascular Health. With a return on investment of 45%, Christiana Care's heart campaign is a resounding success in every measure, including meeting the mission of helping patients both in its community and neighboring states.

Oncology Service Line Marketing

Cancer is the second leading cause of death in the United States, accounting for nearly one-fourth of the deaths in the country. Prostate and breast cancer are the most frequently diagnosed cancers in men and women, respectively, followed by lung and colorectal cancers in both men and in women. Four body regions in particular—breast, lung, prostate, and colorectal—compose nearly three-fourths of all new cancer cases each year. However, hospitalizations for cancer have dropped by almost 10% during the past decade, reflecting a trend toward moving treatment to the outpatient setting.

Female breast cancer continues to dominate the list of payments for treatment of episodes of cancer, as a percentage of all cancer dollars by cancer type. In 2007, for example, female breast cancer crossed the 30% threshold of cancer dollars spent. In second place, colon and rectum cancer spending accounts for about 13% of all cancer treatment spending.

Most service line definitions dramatically underestimate cancer patients' contribution to total hospital revenues and profits. Factoring in cancer patients' high utilization of services such as imaging, diagnostics, and procedures, oncology's true profitability accounts for 13% of inpatient profits and 11% of outpatient profits.

Improved survival rates—the average five-year survival rates have increased from 50% to 63% over the past 25 years—will continue to boost the demand for services, as the number of people living with cancer and requiring medical care will continue to rise, fueling future demand for service.

Cancer patients and family members are information-hungry; even before the Internet they frequented libraries to search out information on treatment options, emerging therapies, and medical experts. Leading-edge treatments, advanced technologies, physician talent, and development of cancer centers of excellence are core areas of focus for organizations. Awards and recognitions (e.g., "Top 100 Hospital" designations) can help reinforce an organization's reputation and achievements, as well. Many cancer programs augment traditional clinical services with complementary therapies to support pain management, stress relief, and mind–body medicine. Some have retail outlets to provide grooming, clothing, and other products to ease the side effects of cancer therapies. Patient experience is critical to creating loyalty and word-of-mouth marketing, as evidenced by the following case study.

Case study: Differentiating on patient experience—Baystate Health System

Baystate Health is an integrated healthcare delivery system serving nearly one million people through three hospitals, outpatient centers, affiliated physicians' offices, and allied health programs in Western Massachusetts. It is one of the largest health systems in New England, with more than 10,000 employees and an annual budget over $1.4 billion. In 2001, Baystate's board of directors approved $39 million to be used to develop a standalone cancer center. While Baystate has a high incidence of cancer in its service area, historically, its oncology services were fragmented. The system's leadership also discovered through consumer research that, of all of Baystate's services, oncology had the highest level of dissatisfaction among former patients.

Armed with that knowledge, Baystate's newly hired physician champion, Wilson Mertens, MD, medical director for cancer services, would help create an exceptional patient experience. Together, with a support team that included marketing leadership and a new oncology administrator, Baystate set out to determine from former patients and families what elements would create a physical, emotional, clinical, and spiritual environment and the best possible treatment experience for patients and their families. Working with Gary Adamson, chief experience officer of Starizon, an experience-design consultancy in

Keystone, CO, the team adopted a theme—"Partners on your Journey of Well-Being"—that became the touchpoint to ensure consistency of message and strategy during the program transformation and facility design process.

The dialogue revealed that families found Baystate's facilities unattractive and unfriendly. They were difficult to navigate and had poor way-finding aids. Business and technical functions were in full patient and public view. Clinically, Baystate's services were fragmented and difficult to access—patients had to navigate through various stages of treatment on their own. The consensus was Baystate offered a cold, unprofessional environment that was uninviting and unpleasant to patients and families, and inefficient for staff.

The cancer program team also interviewed referring physicians in the community about what they looked for in an oncologist and cancer program and their perceptions of Baystate's program versus other local and regional programs. The team hosted retreats with staff, patients, advocates, architects, and donors to design a program and facility that delivered an engaging customer experience. And the team was as inclusive as possible during the program transformation process, involving not only patients and physicians, but also advocates, survivors, and community cancer support groups to advise on facility design, shared resources, programming, and other feedback.

What the team learned through its exhaustive due diligence helped drive the development of a "Center Built by Patients, for Patients." The D'Amour Center for Cancer Care opened in 2005 and ushered in a new era of oncology care that has become a gold standard in the country. Everything—from complimentary valet parking that meant patients didn't have to struggle from the parking lot to the front door, to visual simplicity that relegated business and technical functions out of public view—reinforced a healing environment where patients' needs come first.

With a transformed oncology program and new facility in place, Baystate implemented a targeted marketing plan for oncology services. The goals were to increase patient volumes for the new building, as well as consumer confidence. The message strategy, "Experts in Cancer, Every Step of the Way," aimed to establish awareness for the Baystate Regional Cancer Program, build credibility for the staff as "cancer experts," and bolster consumer awareness.

On every level, the transformed cancer program has been a success. The Baystate Regional Cancer Program ranks in the 98th percentile for "excellent overall quality of care" in patient satisfaction when measured against other programs in the country. Overall volume of all cancer services has grown by 30%, and revenues from facility fees have increased by 35%. Seventy percent of those queried on consumer confidence rate Baystate's cancer services as "best," up from less than 50% before the redesign. And the D'Amour Center for Cancer Care has won numerous awards for facility design, architecture, and patient experience, including the 2008 Discovery Award for Best Patient Experience.

Clearly, crafting a new patient experience that puts families first is a winning service line strategy. Thanks to its due diligence, Baystate has brought a higher level of cancer care to the patients of New England.

Orthopedic Service Line Marketing

Orthopedics—comprehensive joint care, spine, trauma, fracture, and sports medicine—remains one of the more profitable service lines for hospitals, despite increasing technology costs and uneven reimbursement. Joint and spine surgery cases are the most profitable inpatient cases, while sports medicine cases lead profitability on the outpatient side. Three of the top five elective inpatient hospital procedures are orthopedic: knee/hip replacement, back and neck operations, and repair of a previous knee/hip replacement.

Favorable demographics will fuel rapid growth over next decade, with inpatient total joint replacements projected to grow 23% from 2006 to 2016, and outpatient procedures expected to grow 20% in same time period. Sports medicine and hand, foot, surgical spine, and medical spine procedures are also projected to enjoy increased volumes through 2016. The bulk of projected volume growth for sports medicine, foot and ankle, and medical back and spine surgery will occur in ambulatory surgery centers.

Obesity is driving growth in joint replacement surgery in younger patients, with half of all joint replacement procedures now performed on patients under 65.

Needs segmentation can be effectively employed in orthopedic marketing to identify, size, and target prospective patients. Orthopedic service line marketing is frequently niche-oriented, aimed at building volumes for certain procedures. Marketers that consider both preprocedure and postprocedure needs of patients can influence programming and bundling of services such as rehabilitation, pain management, and joint camps, which enable patients who are undergoing similar surgeries to help each other throughout their entire process. Information seminars are a direct-to-consumer selling tactic used by many hospitals, especially for joint replacement or sports medicine.

The following case studies provide examples of how marketing-specialized techniques and focusing on niche segments can increase orthopedic volumes.

Case study: Early adopter—MAKOplasty partial knee resurfacing at ProHealth Care

ProHealth Care, a two-hospital integrated health network in Waukesha, WI, leveraged a breakthrough technology to build on its market position as a leader in orthopedics. MAKOplasty is a robotic arm–assisted surgery that provides implant replacement options for patients with painful osteoarthritis of the knee. The technique partially resurfaces only the diseased portion of the knee, sparing healthy bone and tissue. A partial knee implant is then placed in the joint, allowing the knee to move smoothly and regain more natural knee function again. Because less bone is removed, patients undergoing MAKOplasty can still be considered candidates for other procedures in the future, such as a total knee replacement, if necessary.

ProHealth Care's orthopedics service line director first learned of MAKOplasty during a trade show in early 2009. Excited by the technology, he approached the orthopedic surgeons at Oconomowoc Memorial Hospital with the concept of being the first MAKOplasty program in Wisconsin—and only the 23rd program in the world. The nine physicians were supportive and enthusiastic in their quest to bring MAKOplasty to Wisconsin.

Utilizing a marketing prioritization process and other criteria during ProHealth's annual budgeting cycle, hospital leadership determined that MAKOplasty could be a valuable niche program that yields significant benefits for the system. Marketing leadership gave the green light to the creation of an integrated, multitactic campaign aimed at differentiating ProHealth Care as an innovator in orthopedic care and growing both mindshare and market share.

MAKO Surgical Corp., the manufacturer of the MAKOplasty technology, provided relevant demographic and clinical data. ProHealth's in-house marketing team then used it to create a rigorous consumer-focused marketing campaign directed at men and women, ages 40 to 65, who suffer from early- to mid-stage arthritis of the knee. The campaign launched in late summer 2009 and offered a compelling value proposition, touting ProHealth's "first and only" status with heavy momentum.

Campaign tactics included TV, print, and radio advertising, billboards, Internet promotions, and direct mail. The orthopedists appeared on local TV and radio shows to talk about the procedure, and they participated in live Web chats with the community. Press releases, event sponsorships, and use of social media supported the effort. Outreach to the local Arthritis Foundation resulted in articles in its newsletter and additional exposure for the orthopedists. The campaign was also interwoven into existing marketing tactics, such as the community newsletter, telephone on-hold messages, physician newsletter, and on-site signage.

The value proposition was that MAKOplasty could help patients live their lives again. Patient testimonials were used effectively throughout the campaign. The strategy was to drive potential patients to the existing call center or website, where staff could capture basic demographics and "how heard" insights. Callers were provided with a physician referral along with procedure information. It is important to note that not all patients are candidates for MAKOplasty. Those who are not may be more appropriate for—and directed toward—total joint replacement, providing a significant halo effect and additional volume for ProHealth's orthopedics service line.

Original volume projections predicted that ProHealth Care would perform 50 MAKOplasty procedures in the first year, but patient response was overwhelming: Eight months into the campaign, orthopedic surgeons trained in the procedure had completed nearly 120 MAKOplasty operations. Service line personnel are also starting to track the additional joint replacements that were generated by the campaign. ProHealth Care has made such a successful entry into the market with this breakthrough procedure, MAKO has been proclaiming ProHealth Care's marketing strategy as a gold standard for other facilities adding MAKOplasty to their service mix. Clearly, being an early adopter can help organizations differentiate themselves and capture additional volume as new services and technologies come to market.

Case study: Niche marketing—St. Francis Health System's Geriatric Fracture Clinic

Bon Secours St. Francis Health System operates two acute care hospitals, an outpatient center, surgery center, home care agency, and hospice program in Greenville, SC. The flagship hospital in downtown Greenville has a long history of excellence in orthopedics, including joint replacement, sports medicine, a bone health program, and specialized rehabilitation programs. The Geriatric Fracture Center is the brainchild of one of St. Francis' orthopedic surgeons, who had heard of a similar program in New York. The goal of the program is to get elderly hip fracture patients into surgery as soon as possible after their fracture event to achieve the best possible outcomes and curb the negative effects of bone fractures in the geriatric population.

In most healthcare facilities across the country, hip fractures are considered nonurgent cases, and patients must wait days for surgical care. Fractured bones can cause a tremendous amount of pain, however, which is often managed with narcotics or sleeping aids—both of which can cause delirium in patients. This delirium, in turn, can delay physical therapy, leaving patients with a longer and more difficult recovery. Because patients in the geriatric fracture program are in surgery within hours instead of days, there is rarely a need to use narcotics to manage pain. This means faster and more aggressive physical therapy following surgery, which can lead to a quicker recovery.

Hospital leadership felt the program would be a natural outgrowth of St. Francis' orthopedics program. The development of a geriatric hip fracture center of excellence would enable St. Francis Hospital to strategically position itself in the local market and nearby communities as the geriatric orthopedic center of choice. The program would also improve quality outcomes and facilitate market share growth. According to Bill Munley, vice president of professional services and orthopedics, "Even if the program only broke even, we still felt that it was the right thing to do."

The medical team created a clinical pathway and a fracture center coordinator was hired to help navigate patients through their various stages of care. The marketing plan rolled out in January 2007 and focused heavily on outreach to local emergency services personnel, senior centers, churches, and community centers. Because the program was one of the first of its kind in the country and the first in South Carolina, it also received widespread and enthusiastic attention from the print and electronic media. Follow-up stories continue to spotlight the program, which is also detailed extensively on St. Francis' website and in its community newsletter. A brochure was developed that had a detachable card that reads "Take me to St. Francis," allowing potential patients to state their preference before they ever experience a fall.

Recently, the center was renamed the Osteoporotic Fracture Center to reflect St. Francis' commitment to growing its osteoporosis prevention and education programs. By any measure, the program has proven to be a success. Hip fracture patients at St. Francis receive surgical care much more quickly than the national average—in less than 24 hours as compared to two to three days. Over 70% of St. Francis' patients return to independent living, as compared to a national average of 55%. The average length of stay in the hospital has been reduced from 7.3 days to 3.5 days, and rather than breaking even, the program has increased its contribution margin by 15%.

In just three years, St. Francis has increased its market share in this population from 30% to 40%, well above the hospital's overall market share of 28%. Clearly, St. Francis has carved out a niche that supports its mission and overall brand as an orthopedic center of excellence.

Neurovascular Service Line Marketing

While neurology and neurosurgery disciplines remain relatively low-volume compared to other prominent service lines, demographic trends will steadily and modestly grow the neurosciences patient market, especially for neurodegenerative diseases, cerebrovascular care, and neuro-oncology. Examples include Alzheimer's disease, Parkinson's disease, stroke, epilepsy, and brain tumors.

Many people suffering from brain disease or neurological disorders do not seek or receive the care they need, such as those who have suffered a mild stroke, or those with pain, movement, and sleep disorders. This group represents an opportunity for hospitals to provide community education and patient outreach. Excluding behavioral health, the top neurological diseases or disorders, in descending order, are chronic sleep disorders, stroke, Alzheimer's, epilepsy, Parkinson's, and multiple sclerosis.

Stroke is a growing health problem, as baby boomers age and growing awareness leads to more immediate visits to the emergency department. It is the third leading cause of death and the number one cause of disability in the United States. An estimated 700,000 strokes occur in the United States each year, with an increasing number of strokes occurring in younger individuals.

While stroke is prevalent, it does not compare to those with chronic sleep disorders, which affect about 40 million people a year. Sleep disorder tests are two of the five most common hospital-based outpatient neurology procedures.

Behavioral health, while generally not considered an inpatient service line, has become increasingly connected with the neuroscience discipline as clinical research uncovers biological causes for psychiatric disorders. Inpatient and outpatient volumes dwarf those of every other neurological category.

Neurosurgical services include cerebrovascular procedures, brain tumor treatment, neuro-oncology, and spine surgery. Inpatient neurosurgical service demand is projected to grow about 3% annually, whereas outpatient neurosurgical procedures are expected to grow about 5% per year. Spine care is a significant part of the neurosurgery service line, so much so that some health systems have elevated such care as a separate enterprise. However, spine care is mostly nonsurgical, with 82% of spine-related cases being outpatient pain management. Despite some discussion questioning clinical effectiveness of certain spine procedures, demographic trends, clinical innovation, and physician preference have resulted in robust demand projections. With clinical effectiveness likely becoming a requirement for coverage of services in the future, however, demand for some spine procedures may wane.

Neurosurgical care has traditionally been offered by a select proportion of top-tier institutions because of small patient markets, expensive technology and capital requirements, and a scarcity of qualified physicians.

Case sample: Channel development—Norton Healthcare's Norton Neurosciences Institute

With a network of five hospitals in Louisville, KY, Norton Healthcare (NHC) is the largest healthcare system in the region providing a full range of medical services to the residents of Kentucky and Southern Indiana. The area had recently experienced the closure of several neurosurgery programs and the loss of several neurosurgeons, and was having difficulty recruiting talent. Local residents were often forced to travel outside of the region for some specialized procedures. Yet the need was great: Kentucky is in the heart of the "stroke belt," where brain attack is the third leading cause of death. The state ranks third in the nation in smoking, and sixth in incidence of obesity.

Recognizing the critical demand, NHC launched the Norton Neuroscience Institute (NNI) in 2009, which aimed to bring needed subspecialty services to the region. One key strategy brought NHC's existing neurosurgical group into closer alignment with the system. Another critical effort focused on recruiting fellowship-trained neurosurgical subspecialists from outside the area to help build and augment the neurosciences program at NHC. These included two endovascular surgeons for stroke care, a movement disorders specialist, a pediatric neurosurgeon, and a neurologist specializing in headache and concussion. A total of $100 million to be distributed over 10 years was earmarked for the institute, which would also fund the acquisition of the newest technology and the research and development of a collaborative model. A primary objective was to increase the level of stroke care, achieve stroke accreditation, and decrease the need for local residents to leave the community for care.

When the institute opened in 2009, the marketing team launched a general awareness campaign to create overall recognition for the NNI. Outreach to the physician community was critical to generating awareness and referrals from the medical community. Recognizing the importance of developing new referral channels, two of the newly recruited neurosurgeons took a leadership role in spearheading outreach efforts to the local physician community. Together with NHC's physician relations team, the endovascular neurosurgeons spent three weeks visiting clinicians in 15 different areas in the region. They essentially went door to door, meeting with potential referring physicians and emergency department directors, to talk about the level of care that NHC was now offering and encouraging referrals. The team met with more than 150 clinicians within a 300-mile radius of NHC.

Data proves the visits worked. Within 13 key markets, referrals jumped across the board—anywhere from 13% to 125%, depending on the area—following the visits. Another significant development was the establishment of two clinics in outlying areas of Kentucky and Indiana. Interactions with physicians in these areas underscored the need for the clinics. An NHC neurosurgeon now travels once a month to evaluate patients in those areas. NHC's channel development strategies also included sponsoring a regional conference for physicians. During the program, an actual aneurysm coiling surgery was broadcast live from the NHC operating suite and allowed attending physicians to interact live with the neurosurgeons. In addition, continuing medical education programs were offered by NHC specialists.

Phase two of the marketing campaign to consumers focused on generating stroke awareness. The campaign featured the widow of a local television reporter who had died of a brain aneurysm. She became a key spokesperson and advocate for NNI, and under her leadership, a telethon was held that enabled the system to fund a screening for the community. The March 2010 screening provided MRIs to evaluate aneurysm risk and ultrasounds to detect impending stroke. Of the 600 people who attended, 446 underwent carotid screening for stroke; of these, 39% were found to have some blockage.

Taken together, the referral channel development strategy and outreach to consumers have yielded significant gains in utilization and consumer preference. From 2008 to 2009, NHC experienced a 4% jump in market share in its primary market and a 6.5% increase in its secondary market. Consumer preference grew 7% during that same time. By utilizing focused outreach strategies, NNI is well on its way to meeting its goal of becoming one of the top 10 destinations for neuroscience care in the country.

Women's Health Service Line Marketing

The traditional core of women's health service lines includes obstetrics and nursery, gynecology, breast health, gynecologic oncology, and uro-gynecology. Overall these services account for 26% of inpatient volume and 33% of outpatient volume, with the top procedures being general gynecologic surgeries (e.g., hysterectomy, tubal ligation), breast, OB, and uro-gynecologic procedures (e.g., prolapse, sling suspension). Obstetrics is the primary entry point for most women into a hospital system, and it generates significant volume, contribution, and repeat business. On the national level, every 1,000 deliveries translate into $3.9 million in downstream revenue. Both first-time and repeat C-sections grew rapidly—by 55% and 98%, respectively—between 1998 and 2006. During the same period, the number of vaginal births after C-section (VBAC) decreased by 60%.

The demand for gynecology services and procedures will increase as the population ages. As women get older, the need for uro-gynecology services increases, but less than two in 10 seek help. This latent demand for uro-gynecology services, such as incontinence care, reflects a tremendous market opportunity: 80% of the eligible market are not seeking services.

Many hospital leaders are beginning to think beyond obstetrics and gynecology when it comes to women's health. Because women experience health problems differently than men, addressing women's unique needs now encompasses everything from cardiovascular care to orthopedics to wellness. Heart disease is the number one cause of death in U.S. women, with many deaths attributed to acute myocardial infarction (AMI). Women are also more likely to die from all types of heart attack than men—more than 7% of women die from an AMI compared to 5% of men. Conditions where there is a higher incidence among women than men include osteoporosis, depression, and gallstone disease.

The financial stakes for courting the female healthcare consumer are high: Women control 87% of the spending that feeds health system revenues. Women visit the doctor more often (61%) and fill more prescriptions (59%). Women represent 60% of hospital inpatient and outpatient volumes, generating almost $200 billion in contribution profit to hospital bottom lines.

Increasingly, women's health marketing is less of a traditional service line approach and more of a segment marketing approach executed through service line strategies. Marketers tend to focus strategies on three key areas:

- Service lines that provide for needs unique to women (e.g., obstetrics, gynecology, breast health)
- Niche programs within service lines where disease progresses or presents differently in women, or where approaches in treatment are warranted (e.g., heart disease, cancer)
- Overall positioning and customer experience innovations aimed at building brand preference and loyalty among women

Case study: Meeting the need—Holy Redeemer Maternity Care

Holy Redeemer Hospital serves a mix of urban and suburban populations in southeastern Pennsylvania. While many hospitals in the area have closed their maternity units, Holy Redeemer views obstetrics as an important part of its healthcare ministry and is in the midst of a $10 million upgrade to the entire maternal care unit. It has also built a new, larger neonatal intensive care unit. The hospital introduced its "You're Beautiful, Baby" campaign in 2006 to create a new brand for its maternity services. The goal was to reach women planning a pregnancy within the next year and mothers-to-be with their mobile, active lifestyles and appeal to them with a contemporary campaign focused on the sophisticated nature of the maternity services.

Market intelligence showed that this population was far less likely to read newspapers and highly likely to use public transit such as buses and trains. To launch the campaign, the marketing team placed a heavy emphasis on outdoor advertising vehicles such as billboards, bus sides, rotary panels, and train posters. Banners and posters at local malls also targeted this younger population, and special events, such as "Beach Baby? Maybe!," that were a part of a young women's healthy lifestyles series called "Getting Started," brought the Holy Redeemer message to its target audience. Printed pregnancy guides distributed at these events and through doctors' offices helped provide useful information to moms-to-be while keeping Holy Redeemer top of mind.

Marketing leadership also knew that Holy Redeemer's targeted population was Internet-savvy and relied heavily on the Web when seeking health information. In 2008 Holy Redeemer launched a "You're Beautiful, Baby" microsite that offered a comprehensive online information library through an outside vendor. The site also offered a wealth of other useful applications, such as a baby name finder, baby countdown tool, due date predictor, physician finder, Web nursery, listings of childbirth classes, and animated videos that explained the developmental stages of "Your Growing Baby." Thanks in part to the "You're Beautiful, Baby" campaign, Holy Redeemer's OB market share increased from 16% in 2006 to 23% in 2009, and maternity contacts to the call center increased by 75% during that same time frame.

In 2009, Holy Redeemer launched a Web-based Just4Moms club that allowed the hospital to continue building its maternity services database via the Internet. Again, the marketing team opted for billboards, transit advertising, and event marketing to promote Just4Moms. As part of the club's more aggressive outreach, the marketing team engaged a vendor to create and send weekly e-mails timed to each pregnant woman's stage of pregnancy. Club members will also receive e-mails for up to two years after their delivery, aimed at providing helpful tips on baby's first two years of life and information on the hospital's pediatric services. Initial projections set a goal of 250 club sign-ups in the first year; within six months, membership had exceeded 500 and is currently approaching 1,000.

Since 2005, deliveries are up 60%. Holy Redeemer delivered 3,000 babies in 2009, and is prepared to deliver 4,000 babies annually in the years ahead. By using cost-effective marketing tactics that reach its target market, Holy Redeemer is meeting its mission of linking women in the community with the obstetrical services they need when other facilities have closed their doors to this population.

General Surgery Service Line Marketing

General surgery refers to procedures treating a range of patient ailments, from appendectomy to hernia repair. General surgery is the largest surgical line in terms of volume, has the fifth highest per case profitability, and ranks second in total hospital contribution profit. General surgery is the bread and butter of inpatient hospital services. The top five "profit per case" procedures are tracheostomy, trauma, pancreatic, upper gastrointestinal (GI), and colorectal surgeries.

The site mix of surgeries is expected to remain stable in the near term, with 29% inpatient and 71% outpatient. However, the increasing adoption of minimally invasive procedures is expected to lead to the proliferation of outpatient alternatives to traditional surgical treatments, meaning outpatient volumes will outpace inpatient growth. Overall, general surgery volume is projected to grow more than 12% in the next five to 10 years.

Bariatric surgery accounts for the bulk of general surgery volume growth, and this surgery's contribution profit will overtake trauma and upper GI procedure groups and grow $2 billion over the next decade, with a projected growth of 141%. The increasing prevalence of obesity will also drive growth for plastic (+38%), endocrine (+33%), and transplant (+29%) surgeries.

Referral development is critical to building most general surgery volumes and should be an integral part of the marketing plan. Strategies should focus on developing and communicating systems that make it easy and convenient for physicians and their patients to make timely referrals to specialists and schedule procedures. Communicating patient progress and outcomes with referring physicians is a simple and highly effective loyalty technique. Niche programs targeting both physicians and patients are also effective marketing strategies. Minimally invasive (small incision) surgery centers, weight loss surgery, and gastroesophageal reflux disease treatment are examples of niche programs.

Case study: Niche Marketing—Bariatric Surgery at St. Luke's Health System

St. Luke's Boise Medical Center is Idaho's largest healthcare provider and the flagship hospital of St. Luke's Health System. St. Luke's Boise is known for its centers of excellence in cancer, heart, and women's and children's care. The medical center has been nationally recognized for quality and patient safety and operates the only children's hospital in Idaho.

St. Luke's first began offering bariatric surgery, conducted by one surgeon, in 2001. In 2003, the hospital performed 120 bariatric procedures, demonstrating the heightened demand for the surgery. As part of its commitment to quality, St. Luke's decided to pursue accreditation as a bariatric surgery center of excellence, a designation that was granted in 2006. The designation helped to differentiate St. Luke's from its competition, along with offering a broader range of the types of bariatric procedures. Shortly afterward, the marketing team decided to take a fresh approach to promoting the newly accredited program.

While other programs touted the cosmetic results of the surgery, market intelligence revealed that many patients were concerned about the adverse health effects of their obesity. Many had already developed hypertension or high cholesterol, diabetes, joint pain, and other comorbidities. The marketing team devised a new campaign that used patient testimonials to attest to the new lease on health that patients experienced after surgery and the effects it had on their families. Program leadership also knew that prospective patients did much of their research online before ever deciding on a surgeon or procedure—up to one year's worth of due diligence.

The marketing team devoted considerable resources to enhancing St. Luke's Web presence as a leader in performing bariatric procedures. In addition to building a microsite that detailed the various procedures available and offered animated videos of the surgery and patient testimonials, the hospital ran banner ads on various websites that bariatric patients visited. Billboards and print ads also helped increase awareness of St. Luke's program. Community seminars were important educational and promotional opportunities to reach prospective patients. And notably, the hospital hired a bariatric advocate—and former patient—to follow up with potential patients from the time they attended a seminar until they scheduled their surgery. St. Luke's performed nearly 392 bariatric surgeries in 2009 and has added two more surgeons to meet the increased demand.

In early 2010, St. Luke's added a new interactive component to its bariatric surgery microsite that appeals to this Web-savvy audience. Partnering with an outside vendor, St. Luke's has added jLogs, or "journey Logs," to its website. jLogs are educational videos on what to expect pre- and postsurgery and reinforce the education that all patients must receive prior to undergoing their procedure.

The jLogs are "pushed" to patients once they have committed to the surgery. A dialogue box is provided with each short video segment (under two minutes) to allow comments or invite responses from other patients, often eliciting follow-up from staff at the center. jLogs have also been created using patient testimonials, and a version has been created that the bariatric center surgeons can send to their colleagues to encourage referrals and underscore the capabilities of the center at St. Luke's.

The medical center projects it will perform 425 surgeries in 2010. With the rising tide of obesity in America and St. Luke's Web-savvy approach to promoting its bariatric program, it could well surpass that goal.

Summary

Health systems and hospitals employ different strategies, approaches and methods to position, market, and improve service line performance. Characteristics common across successful service line marketing programs include the following:

- Data-informed decision-making
- A reliance on research to gain insight into customer needs and shape strategy
- Collaboration and shared accountability among operational, clinical, and marketing leaders
- A focus on the details that shape customer experience
- Creative and innovative approaches to 'go to market'

As trends regarding utilization, reimbursement, and demand are ever-shifting in the health industry, it's imperative for service line leaders and marketers to continuously monitor market dynamics and adapt growth and marketing strategies accordingly.

References

"FactFile: Cancer Trends." HealthLeaders Media, July 2009.

"FactFile: Gastroenterology Trends." HealthLeaders Media, December 2009.

"FactFile: General Surgery Trends." HealthLeaders Media, May 2009.

"FactFile: Orthopedic Trends." HealthLeaders Media, April 2010.

"FactFile: Women's Health." HealthLeaders Media, March 2009.

"Heart Disease and Stroke Statistics Update." American Hospital Association, 2008.

Jemal, Ahmedin; Siegel, Rebecca; Ward, Elizabeth; Hao, Yongping; Xu, Jiaquan; Murray, Taylor; Thun, Michael J. "Cancer Statistics." American Cancer Society, 2008.

Mensah, George A.; Brown, David W. "An Overview of the Cardiovascular Disease Burden in the U.S." *Health Affairs* 2007; 26: 38–48.

National Center for Health Statistics. Centers for Disease Control and Prevention, July 2010. *www.cdc.gov/nchs/fastats/default.htm.*

"State Health Facts: Health Status." Henry J. Kaiser Family Foundation, July 2010. *www.statehealthfacts.org/comparecat.jsp?cat=2&rgn=6&rgn=1.*

CHAPTER 6

The Success Formula: Strategy, Leadership, Performance

Service line marketing is a strategic business competency aimed at achieving health system growth and profitability by understanding the needs and wants of customers and meeting those more effectively than competitors. This requires a purposeful, comprehensive, and integrated approach to better understand markets, develop and deliver quality healthcare services, build effective service line delivery models, and create loyal customers.

This has never been more crucial. The new economics of healthcare reform, competition for physician talent, increased merger and acquisition activity, entry of new competitors, and escalating consumer expectations are converging to change the underlying basis for competition and will challenge even the most successful of today's healthcare systems.

Ultimately, service line marketing success will depend more on a health system's vision, strategy, philosophy, relationships, and orientation to the marketplace than to specific tactics to promote clinical programs. To achieve success, health leaders need to develop a market-oriented culture focused on customer needs and a service line structure to deliver differentiated value to the patients, families, physicians, and others that have a stake in the long-term success of the clinical program.

Market Orientation Is Essential

Market orientation is generally defined as an organization's business approach, philosophy, or responsiveness to customer needs and market opportunities—whether its motivations and actions are internally or externally driven. The concept of market orientation is built on pillars of customer focus, quality and service, growth, and financial performance. A health system's capabilities to develop orient marketing toward these pillars depend on the internal structure and culture.

Service line leaders must consider their market orientation and determine whether that approach is congruent with growth aspirations. Marketing capabilities, organizational structure, activities, and investments must then be configured to deliver on the growth objectives.

The following describes different marketing orientations. One approach is not necessarily right where another is wrong. What is important to understand is that each path requires a specific configuration of core competencies, staff capabilities, processes, and investments aligned to organizational vision, strategy, and business objectives to produce results. Misalignment occurs when management wants to achieve significant improvements in strategic growth, for example, but has a production-oriented marketing operation. Consider the following:

- **Product-driven:** A product-driven marketing orientation assumes that as long as a service line has excellent outcomes and a top-notch safety record, business will find its way to the front door. Performance improvement, leading-edge clinical technologies, physician talent, and development of clinical centers of excellence are core areas of focus. Awards and recognitions (e.g., "Top 100" designations) reinforce the organization's quality achievements. Physician influence trumps consumer choice. The clichéd expression "Build it and they will come" is an entrenched belief, as is the assumption that clinical quality alone will create competitive advantage.
- **Sales-driven:** Sales-driven health systems primarily view marketing as a tactical tool or set of tools to drive volume to clinical services or programs. Filling beds, getting appointments, and securing contracts are primary goals. Consumer promotions, physician referral development, and managed care contracting are core capabilities. The focus is on more volume for existing services. These are all good goals, but a purely sales-driven organization may miss opportunities to discover new niches, create new products and lines of business, or enhance points of differentiation that grow overall revenue potential.
- **Market-driven:** Market-driven service lines place greater emphasis on market research to better understand customer needs and discover market opportunities that can be addressed in unique ways. Designing and developing services, programs, and access points to attract key customer segments are priorities for the marketing operation, making research and development a core competency requirement. Marketing

planning is more strategic in market-driven organizations than in sales-driven ones, encompassing segmentation and targeting, product positioning and design, pricing, promotion, and channel strategies—and is a more integrated process through which value is created. Because growing overall market potential and profitability is as important as growing market share, marketers must have a strong profit and loss mind-set.

- **Relationship-driven:** Relationship- or customer-driven organizations place significant emphasis on mass customization as a competency to create one-to-one relationships enabled by sophisticated customer relationship management (CRM) technology that recognizes, supports, and delivers customized messages, offerings, and solutions for valued customers. Today, some of these capabilities are embedded in call center and CRM systems, but new advancements, such as the widespread implementation of electronic health records and growth in social media communities offer health systems unprecedented opportunity to better understand and predict the needs of patients and customers—and proactively design the marketing strategies, tactics, and programs that stimulate and drive demand.

There is one more position to consider: the market-*driving* organization. Market-driving companies are those that reset the rules of competition through value innovation—radical, disruptive moves that create new markets, transform customers into fans, and build such distinct points of competitive advantage that they are difficult to duplicate. Think Apple®, which sold 1,000,000 iPad™ mobile digital devices in less than 30 days after the product launch. Innovation is the core competency—and success comes from developing deep insights into core human desires, discovering unmet needs, and bringing creative, profitable ideas to market.

Complex, competitive dynamics require a market-oriented focus

While service lines have fine-tuned processes and procedures to optimize efficiency, productivity, and profitability—all essential for business success—many struggle to establish the same discipline and competencies for those factors that drive sustainable growth: brand leadership, value innovation, differentiation, portfolio expansion and diversification, customer experience, and channel leadership.

Today, the underlying basis for competition is rapidly evolving, driven by converging forces of healthcare reform, restructuring of the physician services sector, increased consolidations among providers, rising consumer expectations, networked information technologies, the pace of advancements in medical science, and new market entries, including retail, niche, and Web-enabled ventures.

Changing economics are front and center, and make a compelling case for the role that marketers must play in an increasingly competitive industry.

The Service Line Marketer's Call to Action

What are the opportunities for service line marketers? To transform service line marketing from promotions-oriented tactics to growth-oriented strategic leadership. To drive customer value creation and innovation. To build essential partnerships. To crusade for customer-centered practices. To prepare and position service lines for long-term success while enhancing and growing the core business.

As noted in the beginning of this book, the imperative is threefold:

1. Build a service line marketing program that is strategic and focused on near-term growth *as well as* creation of future customers, products, and channels.
2. Establish the critical relationships and linkages across the value chain (e.g., clinical operations, finance, purchasing, IT, physicians, partnerships) to orchestrate alignment with customer needs and service line growth goals.
3. Develop a results-oriented marketing culture and operation that delivers on revenue growth and profit goals.

The marketing success formula for service line marketers, administrators, and physician leaders is embedded in the concepts of strategy, leadership, and performance. How do we identify and seize opportunities for profitable growth? Organize the required talent, resources, and marketing investments? Build an accountable, high-performing, growth-oriented culture? Focused actions create a service line that is marketable, customer relationships that are sustainable, and a marketing strategy that works:

- **Strategy:**
  - Identifying forces of change, understanding competitive dynamics, and discovering opportunities
  - Exploring alternative futures, choosing an overall direction, and articulating strategic growth goals
  - Determining business initiatives and marketing strategies and prioritizing investments
- **Leadership:**
  - Creating leadership will and commitment to strategy-critical ideas and game-changing moves
  - Building the service line capacity, capabilities, and core competencies required for success
  - Forging strategic relationships and partnerships and engaging physicians
  - Developing cross-functional teams that enable effective execution of the marketing strategy
- **Performance:**
  - Creating a bias for action and a market-centric, performance-driven culture
  - Developing implementation plans, accountabilities, monitoring, and reporting systems
  - Aligning goals, incentives, processes, and policies to achieve marketing goals
  - Sustaining the organization's focus and commitment to the plan

Building a Service Line Marketing Culture

A marketing culture is derived from an organizational culture centered on customer needs as well as the sum of organizational activities designed to create profitable exchange relationships by fulfilling those needs.

Lack of ownership across the enterprise for marketing performance will derail success. This happens when marketing is simply viewed as a functional department and not as a core business discipline and competitive competency of the organization.

Service line marketing activities have limited utility when access, capacity, pricing, products, customer service, clinical quality, physician relationships, and other operational aspects of the business are outside the realm of marketing influence. It's critical for the marketing professional, with the CEO and service line leaders, to drive co-ownership of the marketing goals, strategy, and investments—and coaccountability for delivery and performance outcomes—for the entire team.

Healthcare marketers are not alone in struggling to redefine the role of marketing. Across most industries, the rise of global markets, increasing fragmentation and commoditization, revolutionary advances in technology, and changing consumer media and purchasing habits are challenging chief marketing officers to keep up with the pace of market change.

But where to start? The first step is creating a vision for change, and then establishing a new agenda for service line marketing leadership—one that brings marketing into alignment with service line operations to:

- Discover and create service line growth opportunities
- Build strong, differentiated, and defensible service line brands
- Increase overall customer engagement, responsiveness, and loyalty
- Redefine and leverage channel relationships
- Embrace new media, new technologies, and new models
- Establish a culture of progressiveness, innovation, and value creation

Summary

Rapidly changing competitive dynamics make this an opportune time to establish service line marketing as a high-performing, strategy-critical business competency aimed at achieving health system growth and profitability. This requires a purposeful, comprehensive, and integrated approach to better understand markets, develop and deliver quality healthcare services, build effective business models, and attract, create, and retain loyal customers.

References

Corrigan, Karen. "Is Your Approach to Marketing Aligned to Growth Objectives?" Navvis & Company, May 2010.

Dunn, Michael; Halsall, Chris. *The Marketing Accountability Imperative*. Jossey-Bass, 2009.

Kumar, Nirmalya. *Marketing as Strategy: Understanding the CEO's Agenda for Driving Growth and Innovation*. Harvard Business School Press, 2004.

Neumeier, Marty. *The Designful Company*. New Riders, 2009.